Written by Nina Stampfl

Published by Thomas Cook Publishing
A division of Thomas Cook Tour Operations Limited
Company registration No: 3772199 England
The Thomas Cook Business Park, 9 Coningsby Road
Peterborough PE3 8SB, United Kingdom
Email: books@thomascook.com, Tel: +44 (0)1733 416477
www.thomascookpublishing.com

Produced by The Content Works Ltd
Aston Court, Kingsmead Business Park, Frederick Place
High Wycombe, Bucks HP11 1LA
www.thecontentworks.com

Series design based on an original concept by Studio 183 Limited

ISBN: 978-1-84848-319-4

First edition © 2010 Thomas Cook Publishing
Text © Thomas Cook Publishing
Maps © Thomas Cook Publishing/PCGraphics (UK) Limited

Series Editor: Kelly Pipes
Production/DTP: Steven Collins

Printed and bound in Spain by GraphyCems

Cover photography (Che Guevara mural, La Guarida restaurant)
© Nadia Isakova/Alamy

CONTENTS

SYMBOLS KEY

The following symbols are used throughout this book:

ⓐ address ⓣ telephone ⓦ website address ⓔ email
ⓛ opening times ⓘ important

The following symbols are used on the maps:

ℹ	information office	■	points of interest
✈	airport	O	city
✚	hospital	O	large town
⛊	police station	○	small town
🚌	bus station	═	motorway
🚆	railway station	━	main road
✝	cathedral		minor road
❶	numbers denote featured cafés & restaurants	—	railway

Hotels and restaurants are graded by approximate price as follows:
£ budget price **££** mid-range price **£££** expensive

For an explanation of abbreviations commonly used in Cuban addresses, see page 51.

▶ *Ariel view of Havana and its beautiful bay*

INTRODUCING
Havana

Introduction

Cuba's capital is a vibrant Caribbean metropolis with a population of over two million, luring visitors with its colonial beauty and marvellous beaches close to the compact centre. In some ways, a stroll through the historic old town of Havana (La Habana in Spanish) is like a walk through a living museum. Whole streets of colonial buildings and squares, previously abandoned to decline, now appear in new shapes and colours thanks to one of the most comprehensive city restoration projects in Latin America.

That's not all that has changed. Virtually closed to foreign visitors until the 1990s, tourism has been given a boost by the state in order to compensate for the loss of trade with Cuba's major partners in the former Eastern Bloc. Private citizens have opened up *paladares* (restaurants) and *casas particulares* (rooms for rent). So don't expect to be on a forced diet during your stay. Some *paladares* have already gained an international reputation for their innovative blend of creole and international cuisines.

When it comes to nightlife, your expectations can't be high enough. In picturesque Habana Vieja you'll find a plethora of bars, while Miramar is the place for a fancy dinner and in Vedado the night never ends. Live music venues, discos, nightclubs and cabaret shows pump out jazz, trova, timba, songo, Cuban rap and hip-hop, reggaeton... if you thought Cuban music was all about salsa and rumba, think again. Havana, once the key to the New World, desired by the English and Spanish alike, attacked by pirates and corsairs, has it all. After all, what other city allows you to dive into 500 years of thrilling history in the morning and the turquoise waters of refreshingly un-touristy beaches in the afternoon?

◯ *Old cars and vibrant colours are synonymous with Havana*

When to go

Havana's peak season is between December and March, when you get pleasant temperatures and dry weather with the occasional shower. The city is busy, hotels are full and hire cars are difficult to get hold of. Temperatures increase from March onwards and it can get really hot during the summer months.

SEASONS & CLIMATE

Cuba has two seasons, a rainy period between May and October and a dry season from November to April. Between June and October it can get quite stormy, and even dangerous, as hurricanes can pass the island. Temperatures peak at around 27°C in the dry season. Nevertheless, a warm jumper should be part of your holiday wardrobe as cold fronts accompanied by strong winds can hit Havana, especially in January and February.

ANNUAL EVENTS
February
Feria Internacional del Libro An international book fair not to be missed by aficionados of Latin American literature. ⓐ Fortaleza de San Carlos de la Cabaña ⓦ www.cubaliteraria.com

Festival Internacional Jazz Plaza Presided over by Cuban jazz legend Chucho Valdés, the annual festival attracts Cuba's jazz elite as well as top international musicians. ⓐ Teatro Amadeo Roldán & other venues ⓦ www.festivaljazzplaza.icm.cu

Festival del Habano Havana is wrapped in smoke during the festival dedicated to its prestigious cigars. ⓐ Palacio de Convenciones & other venues ⓦ www.habanos.com

April & May

Festival Internacional de Coros Corhabana Enjoy choir music from all over the world or sing along in one of the festival's workshops. The festival takes place on even-numbered years and local tour agencies (see page 134) can help you get involved. ⓐ Teatro Amadeo Roldán & other venues ⓣ (07) 832 4835

◆ *Enjoy the festive spirit of the Zanqueros street performers (see page 131)*

Feria Internacional Cubadisco The Cuban Institute of Music organises this festival, with concerts held at various venues across Havana. Ⓦ www.cubadisco.soycubano.com

La Huella de España Dedicated to Cuba's Spanish roots, this festival is celebrated with a variety of events including dance, folklore, music, cinema and theatre. Ⓐ Gran Teatro de La Habana & other venues Ⓦ www.balletcuba.cult.cu

June

Festival Internacional Boleros de Oro Romantics dance cheek to cheek during this festival dedicated to *boleros*, romantic love songs. Ⓐ Mella, América & Karl Marx theatres Ⓦ www.uneac.org.cu

August

Carnaval de La Habana The Malecón turns into one big party zone during Carnaval with lots of colourful parades, music and dancing.

Symposia de Hip-Hop Cubano Havana's hottest month has some hot Cuban hip-hop music to offer. The festival is organised by the Agencia Cubana de Rap (Cuban Rap Agency) and held in the Casa de la Cultura de Plaza. Ⓐ Calzada no. 7 between 6 & 8, Vedado Ⓣ (07) 8323503

October

Festival Internacional de Ballet de La Habana Havana's Ballet Festival is hosted by the Cuban National Ballet on even numbered years. Ⓐ Gran Teatro de La Habana, Mella & América theatres Ⓣ (07) 861 7391 Ⓦ www.festivalballethabana.com

November
Maratón Marabana Rather hot and humid for a marathon, but running along the Malecón surely makes the torture worth it.
Festival Internacional de Música Contemporánea de La Habana
Contemporary music marks out its space in Havana's festival landscape. ❸ Basílica Menor de San Francisco de Asís & Teatro Amadeo Roldán ⓦ www.musicacontemporanea.cult.cu

December
Festival Internacional del Nuevo Cine Latinoamericano Havana is the host of Latin America's most prestigious film festival.
ⓦ www.habanafilmfestival.com

PUBLIC HOLIDAYS
Triunfo de la Revolución (Triumph of the Revolution) 1 Jan
New Year Holiday 2 Jan
Día del Trabajo (Labour Day) 1 May
Aniversario del Asalto al Cuartel Moncada (Anniversary of the Assault of the Moncada Garrison) 25 & 27 July
Día de la Rebeldía Nacional (National Rebellion Day)
26 July
Inicio de las Guerras de Independencia (Start of Independence Wars) 10 Oct
Navidad (Christmas) 25 Dec
Fin de Año (New Year's Eve) 31 Dec

Havana reborn

It isn't easy for first-time visitors to comprehend the scale of Havana's ongoing restoration programme, but its success is clear to all who live here. Havana's historic centre appears in new splendour, a colonial jewel. To get an idea of what it looked like before work began, just take a walk through the ramshackle streets and alleys of Centro Habana between Paseo del Prado and the Malecón, where ruins, scaffold-clad houses and tumbledown buildings still dominate the cityscape.

Habana Vieja, declared a UNESCO World Heritage Site in 1982, was the first to be declared a Prioritised Preservation Zone in 1993. After the turn of the millennium, the Malecón and Barrio Chino, both located in and around Centro Habana, were included in the conservation zone. The man at the centre of Havana's refurbishment project is popular city historian Dr. Eusebio Leal Spengler. Rather than simply rebuilding, Leal aimed at the 'integral revitalisation' of the historic centre, which includes taking into account residents' welfare. Socio-economic and socio-cultural rehabilitation, such as creating employment and training opportunities, restoring buildings for the benefit of children and elderly people, and building health and cultural institutions, have thus been an important part of Leal's restoration programme. Habana Vieja's newly revamped tourist facilities (hotels, restaurants, attractions) are managed by the state-owned Habaguanex SA, part of the city historian's office. Tourism revenues are directed back into the community.

Plaza Vieja is one of the most emblematic sites in which to visualise the whole process. Before the revolution of 1959, the square had been turned into an ugly, concrete-filled garage. Under Leal's direction, the concrete was carefully removed and one after another the beautiful colonial buildings were restored. If you are lucky enough to come across any 'before' pictures, you'll understand the effort it took to make Habana Vieja look as fantastic as it does today.

⬤ The magnificently restored Plaza Vieja

History

Christopher Columbus set foot in Cuba in 1492 and in 1519 San Cristóbal de La Habana was founded by the Spanish with the celebration of a religious Mass under a ceiba tree on what is now Plaza de Armas. However, it was only after the Spanish had conquered the Aztec and Inca empires, and shipped their looted treasures through the Straits of Florida, that Havana's strategic importance became evident. Pirates and buccaneers, attracted by Spain's treasure-laden ships, cruised the Caribbean. When French corsair Jacques de Sores burnt Havana down in 1555 the Spanish erected various fortifications that still characterise the modern-day city. In 1607 Havana became the capital of Cuba and less than 30 years later the King of Spain declared her 'Key to the New World and Rampart to the West Indies'.

With the increasing importance of sugar and tobacco in the world markets, commerce flourished and Havana experienced a boom in the 17th and 18th centuries. Habana Vieja, surrounded by a massive city wall, took on its present appearance with the construction of majestic palaces and impressive colonial buildings. In 1762 the British invaded Havana, but gave it back to Spain in return for Florida 11 months later. Hurriedly, the Cabaña fortress was raised. Havana became the New World's most fortified city.

The 19th century saw an urban sprawl grow outside the city walls into what is now Centro Habana and Vedado. Chinatown burgeoned when thousands of Chinese were brought to the island to work in the prospering sugar industry. Later than in other Latin American countries, Cuba's desire to cut ties with Spain led to two bloody independence wars. Statues and memorials of war heroes Carlos Manuel de Céspedes, Máximo Gómez, Antonio Maceo and Cuba's greatest national hero, José Martí, politician, thinker, visionary and poet, are scattered all over Havana. Martí's verses have been immortalized in the famous Cuban song *Guantanamera*.

In the first decades of the 20th century Havana erected some of its most distinctive landmarks: the Malecón, the Presidential Palace and the Capitol. In the pre-revolution period, during which there was a strong US influence on the island, the American mafia took control of many of its hotels and turned them into gambling joints. The US-backed general Fulgencio Batista served as president and dictator between 1933–44 and 1952–59, when he was overthrown by the revolutionary 26th of July Movement led by lawyer Fidel Castro with the help of Argentinean revolutionary Che Guevara.

The revolution transformed Havana's destiny. After a period of uncertainty and negotiation, during which the US pressured Cuba with sanctions and the failed 'Bay of Pigs' invasion in 1961, the Communist Party of Cuba was formed in 1965. The party, known in Spanish as the Partido Comunista de Cuba (PCC), is still in charge today, with Fidel Castro as First Secretary and his brother Raúl Castro as President. Under Raúl's leadership, the government's strict socialist policies are gradually being relaxed. When the Soviet Union, Cuba's major trading partner and source of economic support, collapsed in 1991, the country underwent severe economic depression (the so-called Special Period) and was opened up to tourism and foreign investment. Ever since, the 'City of Columns' has attracted millions of visitors, curious to see the fascinating city that seems to have halted in time and at the same time manages to be young, bubbly and innovative.

Lifestyle

It isn't easy to make a living in Havana, with the *libreta* (ration card) granting food for only part of the month and average monthly wages of only around US$20. But Havana's inhabitants have learnt to live with austerity and, most importantly, have lost none of their *joie de vivre*.

🔺 *Sociable Habaneros enjoying a leisurely game*

After the Special Period, Cuba's worst years of economic hardship at the beginning of the 1990s, small-scale entrepreneurship was made legal in some areas. Private citizens could open restaurants (*paladares*, see page 24), let rooms (*casas particulares*, see page 32) or sell art and craftwork. It is not unusual to find medical doctors who are now landlords or sell jewellery in markets. Tourism means money, and that is sorely needed.

Queuing is a part of daily life in Havana and the discipline of locals is impeccable. Whenever a newcomer arrives he or she will ask *¿El último?*, meaning 'Who is the last person in the queue?' It's a good idea to keep this phrase in mind – and whatever you do, don't jump the queue!

Habaneros are sociable folk who love parties and know how to throw a rackety fiesta with roasted pork, rum, dominos, loud music and lots of dancing as standard ingredients. Get-togethers with friends are organised at work, university, on a sidewalk with a CD player and ear-splitting reggaeton, or on the Malecón, Havana's favourite venue for meeting, talking, drinking rum, making music, people-watching and even romance.

Sport is big in Cuba. The local baseball team, the Industriales (see page 30), fills the stadium during home games. As for active sport, the eastern beaches are crowded with city-dwellers enjoying a swim in July and August.

Santería, Cuba's syncretic religion of African origins, plays an important part in the life of many of Havana's inhabitants, especially the Afro-Cuban population. If you pass by a house and hear some drum rhythms it might not be just an ordinary party but a celebration dedicated to a *Santo* (deity).

Culture

A trip to Havana in no way means a 24/7 diet of salsa and rumba. The city's scene is professional, innovative and one of the leading lights of Latin America. The state has done its part in raising Cubans as culture buffs by subsidising all aspects of cultural life and granting artists a first-class education.

The Gran Teatro (see page 65), one of the city's flagships, houses Cuba's National Ballet. The Teatro Amadeo Roldán (see page 81) is the place to enjoy quality performances of classical music. Chamber music performances are hosted by the **Iglesia de San Francisco de Paula** (ⓐ Corner Leonor Pérez & Desamparados) and the Iglesia y Monasterio de San Francisco de Asís (see page 63). Vedado's many theatres put on events of all kinds, from plays, classical music and dance to performances of the famous Conjunto Folklórico Nacional. For a taste of traditional theatre in Spanish head to the **Sala Teatro Hubert de Blanck** (ⓐ Calzada no. 657 between A & B ⓣ (07) 830 1011).

Standing out in Havana's museum landscape is the National Museum of Fine Arts (see page 66), exhibiting works by Cuban artists and old European Masters. If you're more into contemporary art visit the **Centro de Arte Contemporáneo Wifredo Lam** (ⓐ Corner San Ignacio no. 22 & Empedrado ⓣ (07) 861 3419 ⓛ 09.30–17.00 Mon–Fri. Admission charge) or the galleries La Acacia (see page 68) and **Habana** (ⓐ Línea no. 460 between E & F ⓣ (07) 831 4646 ⓛ 09.00–15.00 Mon–Fri). Amateur historians should pop into the Museo de la Ciudad (see page 65) and reserve an afternoon for the Museo de la Revolución (see page 66). The Museo de la Comandancia in the Cabaña fort (see page 63) is dedicated to revolutionary icon Che Guevara.

Hedonistic Havana visitors might choose side trips to the **Museo del Tabaco** (Tobacco Museum ❸ Mercaderes no. 120

⬖ Detail of the Gran Teatro's ornate façade

CUBAN HIP-HOP

Cuban hip-hop originated in the suburb of Alamar, where young black residents became inspired by the rhythms of US hip-hop music and created their own musical blend. The music soon became a way of expressing frustration about the hardships endured in the Special Period. It became so popular that in 1995 the first hip-hop festival was organised – it has since become an annual event (see page 10). Check the programme at La Madriguera (see page 80).

between Obispo & Obrapía ☎ (07) 861 5795 🕙 09.30–17.00 Tues–Sat, 09.30–13.00 Sun. Admission charge) and the **Museo del Ron** (Rum Museum ⓐ Corner San Pedro no. 262 & Sol ☎ (07) 862 3832 🌐 www.havanaclubfoundation.com 🕙 09.00–17.00 Mon–Thur, 10.00–16.00 Fri–Sun. Admission charge).

For Hemingway fans, it's worth making the trip out to the **Museo Hemingway** (Hemingway Museum (ⓐ San Francisco de Paula, Carretera Central km 12.5 ☎ (07) 691 0809 🕙 10.00–17.00 Mon–Sat, 10.00–13.00 Sun. Admission charge) at Finca La Vigía, where the author lived for almost 20 years before leaving Cuba.

Trace Afro-Cuban culture and the origins of Cuba's Santería religion (see page 17) at the **Asociación Cultural Yoruba de Cuba** (ⓐ Paseo de Martí no. 615 between Monte & Dragones ☎ (07) 863 5953 🌐 www.cubayoruba.cult.cu 🕙 09.00–16.00 Mon–Sat. Admission charge).

🔾 *An artisan at work making cigars*

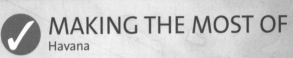

MAKING THE MOST OF
Havana

Shopping

Admittedly not a shopper's paradise, Havana does have its specialities when it comes to retail therapy. In the country of the world's best black tobacco you can of course buy what many experts call the world's finest cigars. Get a box of Cohiba, Montecristo, Romeo & Julieta, H. Upmann, Partagás (the list goes on) at branches of Casa del Habano all over the city. Do, however, note the restrictions on taking them out of the country (see page 128).

Cubans enjoy a fine rum to accompany their cigar. A costly 15-year-old is best drunk neat, whereas cheaper rums are used to mix cocktails such as Cuba Libres, Mojitos or Daiquiris. And, of course, your suitcase shouldn't lack some Cuban CDs. Consider Los Van Van, famous for their songo-salsa, or the reggaeton rhythms of Gente d'Zona or hip-hop sounds of Orishas.

Do as Hemingway did in Cuba and get a *guayabera*, a typical Cuban shirt (linen versions are the most elegant). You can find them at tourist shops or arts and crafts markets around town. Try the **Palacio de la Artesanía** (ⓐ Corner Cuba no. 64 between Cuarteles & Peña Pobre ❶ (07) 866 8360 ⓛ 09.00–19.00 Mon–Sat, 09.00–14.00 Sun) or the Artisan Market (see page 68), the biggest of its kind in Havana. The market also displays various paintings, such as drawings of old American-Cuban cars and naïve paintings of Cuban motifs. For genuine contemporary Cuban art turn to an art gallery such as La Acacia (see page 68) or **La Casona** (ⓐ Corner Muralla 107 & San Ignacio ❶ (07) 861 8544 ⓛ 09.30–17.00 Tues–Sat).

USEFUL SHOPPING PHRASES

What time do the shops open/close?
¿A qué hora abren/cierran las tiendas?
¿Ah keh ora abren/syeran las tiendas?

How much is this?
¿Cuánto vale esto?
¿Kwanto baleh esto?

Can I try this on?
¿Puedo probarme esto?
¿Pwedo probarmeh esto?

My size is...
Mi talla es...
Mee taya es...

I'll take this one, thank you
Voy a tomar esto, gracias
Boy ah tomar esto, grasias

This is too large/small/expensive
Esto es demasiado grande/pequeño/caro
Esto es demasyadoh grandeh/pekenyo/karoh

For nice shoes or clothes pop into **Via Uno** (ⓐ Corner Oficios & Obrapía ⓣ (07) 866 3785 ⓛ 09.00–18.00 Mon–Sat, 10.00–13.00 Sun), **La Bella Cubana** (ⓐ Corner Lamparilla & Oficios ⓣ (07) 860 6524 ⓛ 09.00–18.00 Mon–Sat, 09.00–13.00 Sun) or **Boutique Plaza Vieja** (ⓐ Corner Mercaderes & Brasil ⓣ (07) 864 9514, ⓛ 09.00–18.00 Mon–Sat, 10.00–13.00 Sun), all upscale, stylish boutiques right in the historic centre that are more concerned with quality than with low prices.

Eating & drinking

Back in the dark days of Cuba's Special Period, when sugared water and steaks made of grapefruit skin were part of the Cuban menu, a popular Brazilian *telenovela* (soap opera) triggered an unforeseen gastronomic revolution. It was about a poor woman who starts selling sandwiches and ends up managing a successful chain of restaurants, called 'La Paladar'. It didn't take long for Cubans, inspired by the story, to start selling food from their houses. *Paladares* were born and subsequently legalized in 1994. Innovative chefs started to experiment with traditional recipes, adding new spices, ingredients and flavours. The result is known as Nueva Cocina Cubana (New Cuban Cuisine).

Paladares have enriched Havana's restaurant landscape, which until then had consisted purely of state-run restaurants serving the same old *cocina criolla* (creole cuisine) day in and day out. There are still plenty of these traditional state restaurants and cafés in touristy Old Havana's pedestrianised zones: expect to be served rice and black beans (called *Moros y Cristianos*, or 'Moors and Christians', when cooked together), chicken and pork rather than beef, and seasonal salads and vegetables. Pizzas,

PRICE CATEGORIES

The restaurant price guides in this book indicate the approximate cost of a three-course meal for one person, excluding drinks.

£ up to CUC$10   ££ CUC$10–25   £££ over CUC$25

🔵 *Many a courtyard hides a* paladar *or bar with live music*

USEFUL DINING PHRASES

I would like a table for... people, please
Quisiera una mesa para... personas, por favor
Keesyera oona mesa para... personas, por fabor

Waiter/Waitress!
¡Camarero!/¡Camarera!
Camareroh!/Camarerah!

May I have the bill please?
La cuenta, por favor
La kwenta, por fabor

I am a vegetarian. Does this contain meat?
Soy vegetariano/vegetariana (fem.). ¿Esto tiene carne?
Soy veghetareeyano/veghetareeyana. Esto tyene carneh?

Where is the toilet (restroom) please?
Por favor, ¿dónde está el baño?
Por fabor, dondeh esta el banyo?

I would like a cup of/two cups of/another coffee/tea, please
Quisiera una tasa de/dos tasas de/otro café/té, por favor
*Keesyera oona tasa de/dos tasas de/otro kafeh/teh,
por fabor*

I would like a beer, please
Quisiera una cerveza, por favor
Keesyera oona serbesa, por fabor

(overcooked) pastas and burgers, with fried plantains rather than chips, top the snack menu. There are also a few Spanish, Italian and Chinese restaurants.

Once you move further out to Centro Habana, eating spots become more rare. Head directly to Chinatown, though, and bump into an abundance of cheap Cuban-Chinese restaurants in lively Cuchillo street and the surrounding alleys. *Arroz frito* (fried rice) is the prime Chinese legacy in the Cuban cuisine. Try **Restaurante Tien Tan** (ⓐ Cuchillo no. 17 between San Nicolás & Rayos ⓣ (07) 861 5478 ⓛ 09.00–00.00) for authentic Chinese food.

In Vedado you can find anything from cheap student eateries, bohemian cafés and 24/7 restaurants to first-class *paladares* and elegant, pricey yet good state-run restaurants. The district of Playa, home to most of the city's expats, has plenty of chic dining destinations. Seafood lovers stop by Don Cangrejo (see page 97) or the more intimate **Paladar Vistamar** (ⓐ Avenida 1 no. 2206 between 22 & 24 ⓣ (07) 203 8328 ⓛ 12.00–00.00) – at both of these, sea views come included in the price.

Paladares are usually a bit off the main road, as prime locations in public buildings and pedestrianised zones are reserved for state-run restaurants. In Vedado and Playa they are likely to be found in private mansions. It's a good idea to book in advance if you can.

Tipping is expected and though there are no strict rules a 10 per cent tip is usually adequate. Remember that your waiter will almost certainly be earning a lot less than you, so if you are pleased with your meal and the service don't hesitate to be generous.

Entertainment & nightlife

Havana nights offer more than dirty dancing. Music, however, from salsa to classical, from reggaeton to bolero, and from son to trova, will most likely be a prominent part of a night out.

The area around Obispo (see page 56) is the best for bar-hopping. The live music that emanates from of many bars during the day gets even hotter in the evenings. Just stroll around to see where the liveliest party is going on. For a quieter experience have dinner or a drink in one of the most beautiful (and at night romantic) squares in the historic centre, outside the cathedral (see page 60). And don't forget to reserve one night for the canon shot ceremony at Cabaña fort (see page 63). It's best to arrive there in the late afternoon, explore the whole Morro-Cabaña complex, have dinner at one of the restaurants and then just before 20.30 seek out the best position from which to watch the ceremony.

When the clock strikes midnight and you're in the mood for more partying, think of moving on from the city centre. After midnight there are only a few places (such as the popular Casa de la Musica, see page 73) in Old and Central Havana to continue the fiesta. Vedado has more to offer, including excellent cabaret shows at the larger hotels (see page 86). Usually these places turn into clubs once the show is over, with dancing until dawn. The legendary open-air cabaret show at the Tropicana (see page 99) in Marianao is the place to go if you like this kind of entertainment – after all, it's the original and best. And with a restaurant and cocktail bar on site your evening is booked out.

Jazz lovers have an excellent range of clubs to try out. La Zorra y el Cuervo (see page 89) is Cuba's prime jazz address and the Jazz Café (see page 89), located in a shopping mall opposite the Malecón, is also a restaurant where you might plan dinner with a beautiful sunset view over the Malecón before the concert starts.

If your legs are tired from dancing, take an evening out to watch a film. Cinemas in Havana show films in the original language. Try the **Cine Charles Chaplin** (ⓐ 23 between 10 & 12 ⓣ (07) 831 1101 ⓛ Films: 14.00, 17.00, 20.00 (except for special events) or the **Multicine Infanta** (ⓐ Calzada de Infanta no. 357 between San Miguel & Neptuno ⓣ (07) 870 6526 ⓛ Films: 17.00, 20.00).

Check ⓦ www.cubarte.cult.cu for concerts and fine arts listings and ⓦ http://promociones.egrem.co.cu for popular music.

⬤ The square in front of the cathedral is a fine place for an evening meal

Sport & relaxation

If Cubans aren't playing sport, they'll probably be watching it, listening to a match on the radio or talking about it. There is a long tradition of sport in the country, particularly in boxing, athletics, wrestling and volleyball, and Cuba has produced a lot of world and Olympic champions.

SPECTATOR SPORTS
Pelota
Without any doubt, THE national sport is *pelota* (baseball). When Havana's number one team, the Industriales, play at home the stadium is packed with cheering crowds. In the *esquina caliente* (hot corner) at Parque Central you can usually see groups of Cuban men wildly arguing – but don't worry, they're just discussing the previous night's game. The Industriales are based at **Estadio Latinoamericano** (ⓐ Pedro Pérez no. 302, Cerro ⓣ (07) 870 6526).

PARTICIPATION SPORTS
Basketball, football, athletics
Practise a variety of sports at the public **Ciudad Deportiva** (ⓐ Corner Avenida de la Independencia & Via Blanca, Cerro). The enormous white, coliseum-like structure was built in 1959 and is one of the city's most recognisable landmarks. Opening hours vary depending on the time of year and which facilities you wish to use and there is no central telephone number for information, so it's best just to pop in and see what's on offer.

Diving, snorkelling & deep-sea fishing

Looking forward to submerging yourself in crystalline waters?
Try these organisations:

La Aguja – Marlin Diving Centre ⓐ Marina Hemingway, corner
Avenida 5 & 248, Playa ⓣ (07) 204 5088 ⓦ www.nauticamarlin.com
Centro Internacional de Buceo ⓐ Club Habana, Avenida 5 between
188 & 192, Playa ⓣ (07) 204 5700 ext 406 ⓦ www.cpalco.com

Golf

Golf Club Havana ⓐ Calzada de Vento km 8.5, Capdevila, Boyeros
ⓣ (07) 649 8918 ⓛ 09.30–18.30

RELAXATION

If you're dying to spend a day or two in the great outdoors, it's
only a 45-minute drive from Havana to Las Terrazas (see page 118),
a wonderful nature resort with facilities including hiking trails,
bird-watching, horse-riding and swimming pools.

Spa

Stress release, relaxation and beauty treatments. The Caribbean
provides that anyway – but if you need more, turn to **Spa Club
Comodoro** (ⓐ Avenida 3 & 80, Playa ⓣ (07) 204 5049).

Swimming

A long stretch of sandy beaches awaits you east of the city
(see page 102). Or head westwards for a quick swim at the rocky
beach of Playita de 16 (see page 95). If you like a bit more luxury,
get a daily pass for the posh Club Habana (see page 90).

Accommodation

Havana's hotels range from colonial gems to 1950s-style giants but luckily, over the last few years, a whole variety of classy, charming and snug hotels have opened up in tastefully refurbished mansions in Habana Vieja. Staying here or in neighbouring Vedado has obvious advantages, since you won't really need to bother with public transport or taxis.

If you want something cheaper and more personal, check out the abundance of *casas particulares* (literally 'private houses'), in which you can find a double room for around CUC$25–35 per night. The lower prices here make up for the lack of youth hostels. The quality of *casas particulares* varies from tumbledown townhouses to well-preserved mansions, so be careful when booking. What comes as standard, however, is the experience of real Cuban life and the chance to meet welcoming owners who are a valuable source of information and advice. They can point you towards good restaurants, solve your transport problems or be knowledgeable counterparts for a discussion on the pros and cons of the revolution, if that is what interests you. See Ⓦ www.casaparticular.info or Ⓦ www.casaparticularcuba.org for a good selection.

PRICE CATEGORIES

The ratings on the following pages indicate the approximate cost of a room for two people for one night. Rates in peak season (see page 8) may be higher.

£ up to CUC$70   ££ CUC$70–140   £££ over CUC$140

HOTELS

Hotel Colina £ Choose this friendly hotel if you're looking for cheap accommodation in the nightlife district of Vedado. ⓐ L no. 501 between 27 & Jovellar (Vedado) ⓣ (07) 836 4071 ⓦ www.islazul.cu

Hotel Lido £ One of the very few hotels that can match the prices of a *casa particular*. Simple but cheap and clean. ⓐ Consulado no. 210 between Animas & Trocadero (Habana Vieja & Centro Habana) ⓣ (07) 867 1102 ⓦ www.islazul.cu

⬥ *Hotel Raquel is an art deco delight*

Hotel Lincoln £ Built in 1926, the Lincoln gained temporary fame when motor-racing champion Juan Manuel Fangio was kidnapped from the lobby. His room was rededicated as a museum.  Corner Virtudes no. 164 & Avenida de Italia (Habana Vieja & Centro Habana) ❶ (07) 862 8061 Ⓦ www.islazul.cu

Hotel Deauville ££ A basic hotel with a brilliant location directly on the Malecón, with the Casa de la Música just around the corner. ⓐ Corner Avenida de Italia & Malecón (Habana Vieja & Centro Habana) ❶ (07) 866 8812 Ⓦ www.hotetur.com

● *Colonial splendour at Hotel Florida*

Hotel Florida ££ A colonial beauty located right on busy Obispo street. It has its own restaurant and a piano bar with live music every night. ⓐ Corner Obispo & Cuba (Habana Vieja & Centro Habana) ⓣ (07) 862 4127 ⓦ www.hotelfloridacuba.com

Hotel Raquel ££ Treat yourself: the lobby with its high ceilings, art deco interior, marble floors and columns makes you think you are in a museum. Gym, sauna, massage, a romantic rooftop terrace – is there anything more you would want? ⓐ Corner Amargura & San Ignacio (Habana Vieja & Centro Habana) ⓣ (07) 860 8280 ⓦ www.hotelraquel-cuba.com

Hotel Mercure Sevilla £££ One of Havana's oldest hotels, the Sevilla hosted such illustrious personalities as Josephine Baker and Enrico Caruso. After comprehensive refurbishment it has now reappeared in its former colonial splendour. ⓐ Trocadero no. 55 between Paseo de Martí & Anima (Habana Vieja & Centro Habana) ⓣ (07) 860 8560 ⓦ www.accorhotels.com

Hotel Riviera £££ Travel back in time to the days when Vedado's hotels were controlled by the American gambling mafia. The legendary Riviera was built by mobster Meyer Lansky in 1956 and its lobby still gleams with the original 1950s look. Among the facilities are a swimming pool and the famous Copa Room, a nightclub-cum-cabaret. ⓐ Corner Paseo & Malecón (Vedado) ⓣ (07) 836 4051 ⓦ www.hotelhavanariviera.com

Hotel Tryp Habana Libre £££ This giant, located around the corner from Vedado's lively Rampa street, is managed by the Spanish Meliá hotel chain. With six restaurants (two of them open 24/7), three bars, a swimming pool, beauty salon and shopping area it leaves nothing to be desired. The free shuttle service to the historic centre is extremely useful. ⓐ Corner L & 23 (Vedado) ⓣ (07) 834 6100 ⓦ www.hotelhabanalibre.com

GUEST HOUSES & SMALL HOTELS
Residencia Académica Convento de Santa Clara £ A former convent with dorms of up to six beds is what comes closest to a youth hostel in Havana. Cheap, charming and central. ⓐ Cuba between Sol & Luz (Habana Vieja & Centro Habana) ⓣ (07) 861 3335 ⓔ reaca@cencrem.cult.cu

Hostal Valencia ££ Yet another ramshackle mansion that was turned into a cosy little downtown hotel with only 14 rooms. You can have breakfast, lunch or dinner at Entresuelos in the courtyard, or taste the prize-winning *Paella Hostal Valencia* at the adjacent Restaurante La Paella. ⓐ Corner Oficios no. 53 & Obrapía (Habana Vieja & Centro Habana) ⓣ (07) 867 1037 ⓦ www.habaguanexhotels.com

Hotel Conde de Villanueva ££ This 18th-century mansion was restored to create a haven for cigar aficionados, housing one of the city's best cigar shops. Its nine rooms are located around a beautiful inner courtyard. Guests and non-guests can eat a cheap midday meal at the Cafetera El Corojo or a slightly pricier one at the Vegas de Vueltabajo restaurant. ⓐ Corner Mercaderes no. 202 & Lamparilla (Habana Vieja & Centro Habana) ⓣ (07) 862 9293 ⓦ www.hotelcondedevillanueva.com

Hotel Los Frailes ££ The former mansion of a Cuban noble is now an intimate and quiet hostel. It has only 22 rooms, a most beautiful inner courtyard and an appealing lobby bar. ⓐ Brasil no. 8 between Oficios & Mercaderes (Habana Vieja & Centro Habana) ⓣ (07) 862 9383 ⓦ www.hotellosfrailescuba.com

El Mesón de la Flota ££ Close to Plaza Vieja, this snug inn has a Spanish tavern-style restaurant with tapas and a nightly flamenco show. There are only five rooms, so book early. ⓐ Mercaderes no. 257 between Amargura & Brasil (Habana Vieja & Centro Habana) ⓣ (07) 863 3838 ⓦ www.habaguanexhotels.com

THE BEST OF HAVANA

Culture, history, colonial architecture: there is more to Havana than its truly unbeatable nightlife and beautiful beaches.

TOP 10 ATTRACTIONS

- **Parque Histórico-Militar Morro-Cabaña** Marvel at this gigantic defence complex dominating Havana's bay entrance. The two fortifications, built in different centuries, protected the city against pirates and buccaneers for centuries (see page 63)

- **Capitolio Nacional** Seat of the Cuban Congress until the 1959 Revolution, the grand Capitol is one of Havana's most distinctive landmarks (see page 60)

- **Museo de la Revolución** If you're interested in Cuba's recent history, dedicate some time to this museum in the former Presidential Palace (see page 66)

- **Fábrica de Tabacos Partagás** Guided tours at this cigar factory show you the art of making Cuba's most prestigious product (see page 60)

- **Plaza Vieja** Surrounded by beautifully renovated colonial buildings, this square is one of the best places in Havana to enjoy a relaxing drink (see page 64)

- **El Malecón** Cuba's famous seaside avenue, lined with newly refurbished and tumbledown buildings, is filled every evening with crowds of sociable Habaneros (see page 78)

- **Playas del Este** A long stretch of white sand beaches and turquoise waters, only 20 minutes from the centre (see page 102)

- **Casa de la Música Centro Habana** One of the city's finest live music venues, with concerts most nights and matinées in the afternoon (see page 73)

- **Callejón de Hamel** This colourful alley in Centro Habana, with murals by an Afro-Cuban artist and live rumba on Sundays, is one of the best ways to experience the city's Afro-Cuban soul (see page 42)

- **Valle de Viñales** The 'Garden of Cuba' and a natural paradise waiting to be explored (see page 120)

⬤ *Havana's landmark building, the Capitolio Nacional*

Suggested itineraries

HALF-DAY: HAVANA IN A HURRY
Walk from Plaza Vieja (see page 64) along Mercaderes and marvel at the colonial architecture. After a tour around Plaza de Armas,

● *Enjoy the view from the roof terrace of Hotel Ambos Mundos*

which contains some of the city's most emblematic historic buildings, have a quick coffee on the roof of Ambos Mundos (see page 71) while enjoying the view over the city. Stroll along Obispo and Paseo del Prado before taking a coco taxi along the Malecón (see page 78).

1 DAY: TIME TO SEE A LITTLE MORE

After a walk through Habana Vieja, treat yourself to a quick coffee or daiquiri at Hemingway's old haunt El Floridita (see page 73), then take a taxi to the Morro-Cabaña complex (see page 63). Have lunch in one of the restaurants there and enjoy the marvellous views. Head back to the centre for a matinée concert at the Casa de la Música Centro Habana (see page 73).

2–3 DAYS: TIME TO SEE MUCH MORE

Visit the National Museum of Fine Arts (see page 66) and after lunch on Plaza Vieja buy some souvenirs at the Artisan Market (see page 68) in the harbour. Book a table at one of the *paladares* in Miramar (see page 90), preferably one with a sea view. Join a guided tour at the Partagás factory (see page 60), and make sure you spend at least an afternoon at Santa María del Mar beach (see page 109).

LONGER: ENJOYING HAVANA TO THE FULL

Plan a trip to the Viñales Valley (see page 114) and make a stop in Las Terrazas (see page 118), Cuba's first eco-tourism resort with hiking, horse-riding and swimming in cool natural waters. Back in the city combine culture with the pleasures of Havana's nightlife: cabarets, jazz clubs, theatres, cinemas and nightclubs.

Something for nothing

Cuba has two currencies, the Cuban Peso (CUP), also known as the *moneda nacional* (national currency), and the Cuban Convertible Peso (CUC), which is roughly equal to a US dollar and is known colloquially as *chavitos*. The CUC is used in hotels, tourist restaurants and almost all shops, while the CUP is used by locals for staple goods. However, change some of your CUC into CUP, then wander through Havana and see what you can get for the equivalent of just a few US$ cents (even if this entails standing in a queue for some time). Note that both currencies carry the dollar symbol which may lead to some confusion.

Start off with a coffee just as Cubans like it: small, black and strong, at **Café Habana** (❷ Corner Mercaderes & Amargura ◷ 08.00–19.00) – it costs just one peso (about five CUC centavos) for a tasty cup. Have a snack at one of the stands in Obispo, where a piece of pizza or a hot dog costs you ten pesos (CUC$0.50). Then head to Callejón de Hamel, between Aramburu and Espada. This little Centro Habana alley is one of the centres of Afro-Cuban culture. It owes much of its fame to Salvador González Escalona, an Afro-Cuban artist whose first outdoor murals can be admired here. Colourful and vibrant, it gets even hotter on Sundays at 11.00 when live rumba sessions start with heavy drum rhythms and dancing. Any other day you'll have free concerts with bands striking up in almost every bar or restaurant in tourist areas.

Only the brave and very, very patient plan a trip to the beach by bus, but if you do it costs only two pesos (as opposed to more than CUC$30 for a round trip by cab). Take bus no. 400 to Guanabo. If you're not into swimming, you might at least cool down with ice cream at Coppelia (see page 83). You'll have to wait in the 'national currency queue' together with locals, but once inside you're rewarded with Cuba's best ice cream for less than a quarter of a CUC$. No evening programme so far? Go to the pictures (see page 29), which will cost you two or three pesos (less than 15 CUC centavos). Spend the time before the film starts on the Malecón and watch the coming and goings while enjoying the lively atmosphere at sunset.

⬤ *A local favourite – the Coppelia ice cream parlour*

When it rains

No need for you to cry if the Caribbean sky above you cries – there's plenty to do in Havana on rainy days. Stock up on souvenirs at Havana's biggest artisan market (see page 68), housed in a (covered) harbour warehouse. Or take the opportunity to visit the museums you planned to see. The National Museum of Fine Arts (see page 66) and the Revolution Museum (see page 66) are within a short walk of one another so you won't get very wet in between.

The Rum Museum (see page 20) not only demonstrates the art of making rum but allows you to sip a few samples. And if that doesn't cheer you up, give the **Museo del Chocolate** (Chocolate Museum ⓐ Corner Amargura & Mercaderes ⓛ 09.00–20.00) a chance to sweeten your day. A visit to Partagás cigar factory (see page 60) is another possibility, where you can watch cigars being made.

Any day is a good day to go to a matinée concert and get crazy on the dance floor, but a rainy day – even better! The city's hottest live music venues, the Casas de la Música in Central Havana and Miramar (see pages 73 & 100), the Diablo Tun Tun (see page 100), as well as the Café Cantante Mi Habana and the Piano Bar Delirio Habanero (see pages 86 & 89) offer afternoon concerts. Cheaper than the evening performances, they are often attended by more locals, making it an even more authentic experience. If the dancing inspires you, it's easy to arrange a couple of dance lessons with a private teacher.

And if the rain looks like it's setting in for the day, book a table at one of Havana's top restaurants and splash out on a long, lazy, fabulous meal.

⬥ *Explore the city's treasures out of the rain at the Museum of Fine Arts*

On arrival

TIME DIFFERENCE

Havana is five hours behind Greenwich Mean Time (GMT).
Between mid-March and the end of October, clocks are put
forward by one hour for Daylight Saving Time. During that
period, Havana is four hours behind GMT.

ARRIVING

By air

José Martí International Airport (🅰 Avenida Van Troi & Final,
Boyeros 🕐 (07) 642 0100 or 275 1200) is located about 20 km
(12½ miles) southwest of Havana and is connected to destinations
in Europe, Canada, Latin America and the Caribbean (see page 126).
The airport has taxis, tourist information, car rental services,
buses to other provinces, an exchange office, internet access,
airline offices, a café and various souvenir shops.

There is no public transport connecting the airport with the
city. Taxis currently charge about CUC$20–30 for a ride to different
parts of the city. Confirm the price with the driver before getting
in the car.

Some cheap charter flights arrive at **Juan Gualberto Gómez
International Airport** (🅰 Avenida Mártires de Barbados km 5,
Varadero, Matanzas 🕐 (045) 253 612 or 247 015), 134 km (83 miles)
northeast of Havana. There is a good bus connection to Havana
from here, with buses leaving four times a day in both directions.
The journey takes nearly three hours and costs CUC$10.80 one way.

🔘 *Estación Central – Havana's central station*

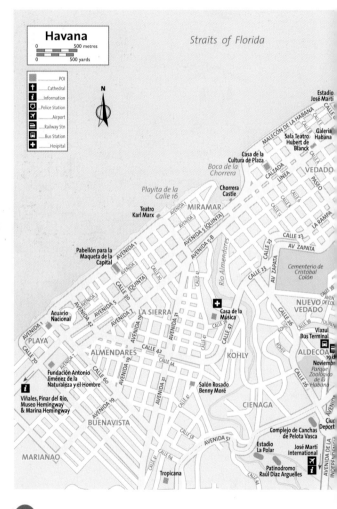

Havana

0	500 metres
0	500 yards

	POI
	Cathedral
	Information
	Police Station
	Airport
	Railway Stn
	Bus Station
	Hospital

N

Straits of Florida

Estadio José Martí

MALECÓN DE LA HABANA

Galeria Habana

Sala Teatro Hubert de Blanck

Casa de la Cultura de Plaza

CALZADA

VEDADO

LINEA

PASEO

Boca de la Chorrera

Chorrera Castle

Playita de la Calle 16

Teatro Karl Marx

MIRAMAR

AVENIDA 1

AVENIDA 3

AVENIDA 5 (QUINTA)

AVENIDA 5-B

LA RAMPA

CALLE 23

AV ZAPATA

CALLE 23

Pabellón para la Maqueta de la Capital

AVENIDA 1

AVENIDA 3

CALLE 28

CALLE 30

Río Almendares

CALLE 41

Cementerio de Cristóbal Colón

NUEVO VEDADO

Acuario Nacional

AVENIDA 5

AVENIDA 7

LA SIERRA

AVENIDA 19

AVENIDA 31

Casa de la Música

CALLE 26

KOHLY

Viazul Bus Terminal

PLAYA

AVENIDA 1

CALLE 70

ALMENDARES

AVENIDA 19

CALLE 42

CALLE 44

KOHLY

ALDECOA

19 d Noviembre

Fundación Antonio Jiménez de la Naturaleza y el Hombre

CALLE 60

AVENIDA 31

Salón Rosado Benny Moré

Parque Zoológico de la Habana

Viñales, Pinar del Río, Museo Hemingway & Marina Hemingway

CIENAGA

BUENAVISTA

AVENIDA 19

CALLE 58

Ciuc Deport

MARIANAO

CALLE 41

CALLE 64

AVENIDA 51

Complejo de Canchas de Pelota Vasca

Estadio La Polar

José Martí International

AVENIDA DE LA INDEPENDENCIA

Tropicana

CALLE 72

Patinodromo Raúl Díaz Arguelles

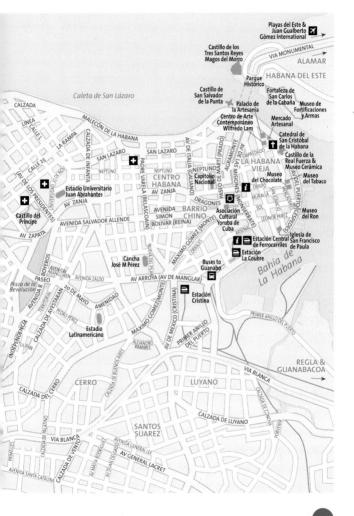

By rail

Havana's Estación Central and Estación La Coubre are linked to Santiago, Matanzas and other cities in Cuba, but train travel is not recommended for visitors due to the likelihood of long delays and unsanitary conditions.

By road

Havana is connected to other provinces by an efficient long-distance bus service operated by Víazul. In Havana buses arrive at and leave from the **Víazul Bus Terminal** (ⓐ Avenida 26 & Zoológico, Nuevo Vedado ⓣ (07) 881 1413 ⓦ www.viazul.cu).

FINDING YOUR FEET

Havana is probably the safest city in Latin America, so you can walk around relaxed. However, take the usual precautions that you would in any bigger city. Female and male hustlers (*jineteras* and *jineteros*) may try to attach themselves to tourists and can be a bit insistent, especially in touristy areas, bars and nightclubs. However, if you show them a determined cold shoulder they will back off.

ORIENTATION

Havana is divided into 15 *municipios* (districts). The areas of tourist interest are located in the north, on the coastline with the Straits of Florida, with a small natural bay lying in the city centre. The historic centre, to a large degree identical to Habana Vieja, is located on the eastern coast of Havana Bay. A tunnel through the bay connects Habana Vieja with the forts opposite the bay, which are officially part of Habana del Este (Eastern Havana).

FINDING YOUR WAY

Street names in Habana Vieja and Centro Habana take some getting used to. Many streets have two names. Locals widely prefer the old names and might even not know the official street names. City maps sold in Havana give the official names with the old names in brackets. In Vedado, street names are generally given as numbers and letters (e.g. Corner 17 & E, which means at the corner of 17th street and E street). In Playa, avenues and streets are a mere grid of numbers (e.g. Avenida 5 between 188 & 192, which means it's on 5th avenue between streets 188 and 192).

In Spanish, *esquina* (often abbreviated to esq) means 'corner' and *entre* (abbreviated to e/) means 'between'. *Calle* means 'street', while *avenida* is simply 'avenue'. You will sometimes see Avenida 1 written as 1ra (short for Spanish *primera*, or 'first'), 5 written as 5ta (*quinta*, or fifth), and 7 written as 7ma (*séptima*, or seventh) and so on.

This is also the way to get to the Playas del Este Playas del Este.

West of Habana Vieja, you will come across (in this order) Centro Habana, Vedado and Miramar, which is part of Playa. The Almendares river forms a natural border between Vedado and Miramar.

A good way to get your bearings on arrival is to take the **HabanaBus Tour** (ⓦ www.transtur.cu), a tourist bus service offering round trips through the city on three routes, with stops at tourist sights, major hotels, bars and restaurants.

IF YOU GET LOST, TRY ...

Excuse me, do you speak English?
Disculpe, ¿usted habla ingles?
Deescoolpeh, oosted ablah eengles?

Excuse me, is this the right way to the old town/the city centre/the tourist office/the station/the bus station?
Disculpe, ¿este es el camino correcto hacia el centro histórico/el centro de la ciudad/la oficina de turismo/ la estación de trenes/la estación de guaguas?
Deescoolpeh, este es el kameeno korrekto asya el sentro eestoreekoh/el sentro de la ceeydad/la ofiseenah de tooreesmoh/la estasyon de trenes/la estasyon de gwa-gwas?

Can you point to it on my map, please?
Por favor, ¿lo puede indicar en mi mapa?
Por fabor, loh pwede eendeekar en mee mapa?

GETTING AROUND

Public transport in Havana is anything but reliable and efficient. Although it has slightly improved over recent years, even locals often resort to official taxis paid in CUC and so-called *colectivos*, old American cars operating as shared taxis and paid in Cuban pesos. When buses finally arrive after a long wait they are usually overcrowded and make for an uncomfortable ride.

Habana Vieja is easy to get around on foot since most of its

sights are located within walking distance of one another.
For other distances, you'll have to take a taxi. In Centro Habana
you'll see two-seater bicycle taxis known as Bici-taxis. Although
they're not officially allowed to transport tourists you might still
be able to catch one for a short distance – but note they may
take a longer route to avoid the policed areas of the city. Locals
pay in CUP but they'll charge you in CUC, so negotiate a price
beforehand. **Coco taxis** (☏ (07) 877 5762) are yellow coconut
shell-type motor scooter taxis with two seats at the back.

◆ *Coco taxis are a fun way to get around the city*

You can hail them in the streets of touristy areas (or they'll hail you). When empty, they honk their horn to attract attention.

There are also 'proper' taxis, differing a bit in quality. Old Ladas are the cheapest, but it might be that one of the doors doesn't open, or a window doesn't close properly (air-conditioning is a dream). Modern cars with standard comforts are more expensive. In any case always check if there's a functioning meter. You can hail a cab in the street, if you can find an empty one, or catch them outside upscale hotels. You can also order one by calling ☎ (07) 855 5555.

As there is no efficient public transport to the Playas del Este (except for one Víazul bus stopping in Guanabo in the early morning and returning late in the evening) you will probably have to take a taxi. Viñales and Pinar del Río city are connected with Havana by a Víazul bus, but the service is not frequent. However, various travel agencies (see page 134) offer one-day excursions to the best out-of-town destinations.

CAR HIRE

If you're planning to stay in Havana, getting around by taxi is cheaper than renting a car. If you plan various trips to the Playas del Este and out of town, though, hiring a car is worth it and allows you more freedom. Note that in peak season (late December to early January) many agencies virtually run out of cars. The state-run **Transtur** (📍 L no. 2502 between 25 & 27, Vedado ☎ (07) 835 0000 🌐 www.transtur.cu) operates a network of offices through its brands Cubacar, Havanautos and Rex, the latter for luxury cars.

◗ *Interior of the Capitolio Nacional*

THE CITY OF
Havana

Habana Vieja & Centro Habana

Havana's historic centre, consisting of Habana Vieja (Old Havana) and its fortifications, has been a UNESCO World Heritage Site since 1982. It is, without doubt, one of the most beautiful examples of colonial architecture in the Americas. Street by street and building by building, renovation is an ongoing project (see page 12), with classy hotels, stylish cafés and trendy boutiques opening up all over the area. The Spanish colonial core of the old town contains the city's most important historic buildings and is a wonderful place in which to stroll around and enjoy its architectural beauty and rich historical and cultural heritage. It is no museum piece but a living, breathing, vibrant and authentic city.

Things get even more lively in Centro Habana, home to Chinatown and a part of the Malecón. Streets such as the Avenida de Italia (Galiano) and San Rafael are some of its most emblematic thoroughfares.

SIGHTS & ATTRACTIONS

Calle Obispo & Plaza de Armas

Dive straight into the heart of Havana's street life in this narrow, pedestrianised street full of shops, hotels, restaurants, noisy bars blasting out live music and busy Habaneros. At no. 407–411 there is a fun arts and crafts market. Plaza de Armas is surrounded by Spanish colonial buildings: the Palacio de los Capitanes Generales (now housing the City Museum, see page 65), Palacio del Segundo

▶ *Colourful Calle Obispo*

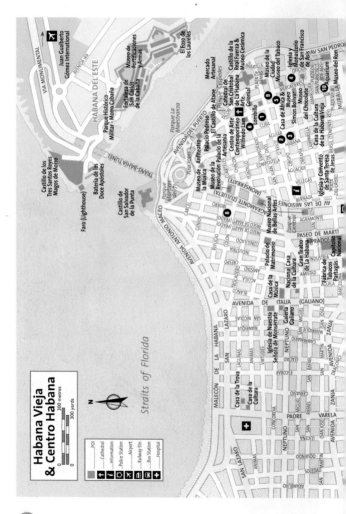

Habana Vieja & Centro Habana

0 — 300 metres
0 — 300 yards

N

Straits of Florida

Legend
- POI
- Cathedral
- Information
- Police Station
- Airport
- Railway Stn
- Bus Station
- Hospital

Juan Gualberto Gómez International

VIA MONUMENTAL

HABANA DEL ESTE

Museo de Fortificaciones y Armas

Fortaleza de San Carlos de la Cabaña

El Foso de los Laureles

Parque Histórico Militar · Morro Cabaña

Parque La Maestranza

Mercado Artesanal

Castillo de la Real Fuerza & Museo Ceramica

Castillo de San Cristóbal

Museo de la Ciudad

Museo del Tabaco

Castillo de los Tres Santos Reyes Magos de Morro

Iglesia y Monasterio de San Francisco de Asís

AV SAN PEDRO

Museo de Arte Colonial

Catedral de La Habana

Casa de Africa

Museo del Chocolate

Casa de la Cultura de la Habana Vieja

Aquarium

Museo del Ron

Bateria de los Doce Apóstoles

Faro (lighthouse)

Castillo de San Salvador de la Punta

TRANS-BAHIA-TUNEL

Palacio Pedroso

Casa de Asia

Simon Bolivar

Iglesia y Convento de Santa Teresa

AVENIDA DEL PUERTO

Centro de Arte Contemporáneo de Wilfredo Lam

El Castillo de Atane

Centro de Arte Artesania

Lombillo

Museo de la Revolución Palacio de la

Museo de la Música

Museo de Amfiteatro

Parque Martires del 71

AVENIDA ANTONIO MACEO

Museo Nacional de Bellas Artes

AV DE LAS MISIONES

SACRAMENTE (ZULUETA)

Palacio de Matrimonio

Nacional Casa de la Música

Casa de la Cultura

Parque Central

PASEO DE MARTI (PRADO)

Gran Teatro de La Habana

Capitolio Nacional

Fábrica de Tabacos Partagás

AVENIDA DE ITALIA (GALIANO)

Galería Galiano

Iglesia de Nuestra Señora de Monserrate

MALECÓN DE LA HABANA

Casa de la Trova

Casa de la Cultura

NEPTUNO

58

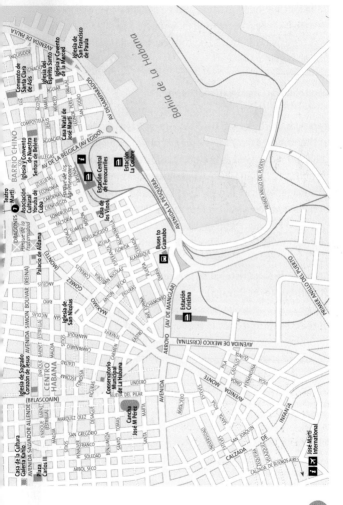

Cabo (ancient headquarters of the Spanish vice-governor), Castillo de la Real Fuerza and El Templete (the site where the first Mass was celebrated on the occasion of Havana's foundation in 1519).

Capitolio Nacional (National Capitol)
Built in 1926, Havana's (slightly taller) version of Washington's Capitol is worth a visit. The Salón de los Pasos Perdidos (Room of the Lost Steps) contains a gigantic bronze female Statue of the Republic, as well as the 'point zero diamond' from which all distances between Havana and other places in the country are calculated. You can also see the library and former chamber of the Senate on a guided tour. One of Havana's few internet cafés can be found here. ⓐ Paseo de Martí between San José & Dragones ⓣ (07) 863 7861 ⓛ 09.00–17.00. Admission charge

Catedral de San Cristóbal de la Habana (Cathedral of St Christopher of Havana)
A baroque construction flanked by two unequal towers, this is one of the oldest cathedrals in the Americas. After a comprehensive refurbishment in the 19th century, the interior now appears in neoclassical style. The square in front contains other fascinating baroque buildings and is a romantic spot at dusk. ⓐ Plaza de la Catedral, corner San Ignacio & Empedrado ⓣ (07) 861 7771 ⓛ 09.00–17.00 Mon–Sat, 09.00–12.30 Sun (times vary)

Fábrica de Tabacos Partagás (Partagás Cigar Factory)
The Partagás factory, located right behind the Capitol, offers tours for all those interested in learning about the art of rolling

⬥ *The grand Capitolio Nacional*

◆ *Church & Monastery of St Francis of Assisi*

cigars. Connoisseurs can enjoy some of the finest *puros*, as locals call their prestigious tobaccos, in the stylish smokers' lounge. ⓐ Industria no. 520 between Barcelona & Dragones ⓣ (07) 862 4604 ⓛ 09.00–11.00, 12.00–13.30 Mon–Fri. Admission charge (paid in advance at hotel tourism desks only)

Iglesia y Monasterio de San Francisco de Asís (Church & Monastery of St Francis of Assisi)

Enthusiasts of classical and chamber music should try to catch a concert at this church-turned-concert hall, which has brilliant acoustics. At the entrance is a bronze statue of the Caballero de Paris (Gentleman from Paris), a charismatic, educated, homeless man who gained fame wandering through Havana's streets in the 1950s and engaging passers-by in philosophical discussions. ⓐ Plaza de San Francisco de Asís ⓣ (07) 862 9683 ⓛ 09.30–17.00 Mon–Sat

Parque Histórico-Militar Morro-Cabaña (Morro-Cabaña Historical Military Park)

You'll need some time to explore this huge military complex, which contains the Castillo de los Tres Santos Reyes Magos del Morro (Morro Castle), finished in 1630, and the Fortaleza de San Carlos de la Cabaña (San Carlos de la Cabaña Fort), built almost one and a half centuries later to cover a gap in the city's defence system. Don't miss the *cañonazo* (canon shot) ceremony at the Cabaña, held daily at 20.30, which in the past marked the closing of the city gates. ⓐ Habana del Este ⓣ Morro: (07) 863 7941; Cabaña: (07) 862 0617 ⓛ Morro: 08.00–20.00; Cabaña: 10.00–23.00. Admission charge

⬤ *Learn the art of rolling cigars at the Partagás Cigar Factory*

Paseo de Martí (Paseo del Prado/El Prado)

Laid out in the late 18th century, Paseo del Prado (now officially called Paseo de Martí) was designed to lend Havana some of the flair of the grand European boulevards. Take time out on the shady stone benches and study the beautiful buildings; note those with Moorish influence in particular. The best time to stroll along here is in the early evening, when families and friends gather for the Cuban equivalent of the *passeggiata*.

Plaza Vieja

The best example of the success of Havana's restoration project (see page 12). The 'Old Square', which dates back to the 16th century, was distorted by an ugly car park before the revolution but now appears in new splendour thanks to careful renovation works.

CHINATOWN

Havana's Barrio Chino isn't as big, lively, authentic or colourful as the Chinatowns of US cities. In fact most of the Chinese, who came to Cuba to work as *macheteros* (sugar cane cutters) after the abolition of slavery, emigrated to the US after the revolution. Although still rather run-down, its potential as a tourist attraction has become evident and the area is now undergoing restoration. Locals flock there for its cheap eateries that serve food in abundance.

CULTURE

Gran Teatro de la Habana (Grand Theatre of Havana)

Located at the Centro Gallego building, this is the seat of Cuba's National Ballet and National Opera. If you can, catch Cuba's world-famous ballet company in a performance choreographed by legendary ballerina Alicia Alonso. ⓐ Corner Paseo de Martí & San Rafael ⓣ (07) 861 7391 ⓦ www.balletcuba.cult.cu ⓑ Box office: 14.00–20.00

Museo de la Ciudad (City Museum)

Travel back in time to Havana's colonial days at this interesting museum at the Palacio de los Capitanes Generales. Displays of furniture, porcelain, crystal and paintings depict various episodes of the city's history, including the independence wars, the period of US influence on the island and the sinking of US warship *Maine*

in Havana's harbour. @ Tacón no. 1 between O'Reilly & Obispo
🕿 (07) 861 5001 🕒 09.30–17.00 Tues–Sun. Admission charge

Museo Nacional de Bellas Artes (National Museum of Fine Arts)
This excellent museum's two major collections, one for Cuban
and one for international art, are housed in separate buildings
and both are worth visiting.
Colección de Arte Cubano (Cuban art) @ Trocadero between
Agramonte & Avenida de las Misiones 🕿 (07) 861 3858
🕒 10.00–18.00 Tues–Sat, 10.00–14.00 Sun
Colección de Arte Universal (International art) @ Corner Agramonte
& San Rafael 🕿 (07) 863 9484 🕸 www.museonacional.cult.cu
🕒 10.00–18.00 Tues–Sat, 10.00–14.00 Sun. Admission charge

Museo de la Revolución (Revolution Museum)
It's not only history enthusiasts who will enjoy a tour through
this museum, housed in the former presidential palace. You can
take a photo of yourself in front of revolutionary heroes Che
Guevara and Camilo Cienfuegos, exhibited in Madame Tussauds
style. Behind the museum, the Granma Memorial depicts the
yacht that brought Fidel Castro and his 81 revolutionaries from
Mexico to Cuba in 1956. @ Refugio no. 1 between Agramonte
& Avenida de las Misiones 🕿 (07) 862 4091 🕒 10.00–18.20.
Admission charge

RETAIL THERAPY

Casa del Habano Purchase the best Cuban cigars or just have
a puff and a drink at the adjacent Smokers' Club. @ Hotel

⬥ Cuban cars and tanks outside the Revolution Musuem

Conde de Villanueva, corner Mercaderes no. 202 & Lamparilla
🕿 (07) 862 9293 🌐 www.lacasadelhabano.cu 🕒 09.00–19.00

Galería La Acacia Art buffs come here to buy contemporary
Cuban art. 📍 San José no. 114 between Industria & Consulado
🕿 (07) 861 3533 🌐 www.galeriascubanas.com 🕒 09.00–17.00
Mon–Thur, 09.00–16.00 Fri & Sat

Libreros de la Plaza de Armas Looking for a copy of *El Diario del
Che en Bolivia (Bolivian Diary of Ernesto Che Guevara)* or Fidel
Castro's *La Historia Me Absolvera (History Will Absolve Me)*?
This second-hand book market is the place to find them.
📍 Plaza de Armas 🕒 09.00–18.00 Mon–Sat

Longina Música The selection of CDs is one of the best in town
and if you're taken with Afro-Cuban rhythms get yourself some
bongos! 📍 Obispo no. 360 🕿 (07) 862 8371 🕒 10.00–18.00
Mon–Sat, 10.00–13.00 Sun

Mercado Artesanal (Artisan Market) Havana's biggest
handicraft market is the usual mix of beautiful craftwork and
some obligatory kitsch. Browse for *guayaberas* (typical Cuban
shirts), paintings, elaborate jewellery boxes, shell earrings and
much more. 📍 Centro Cultural Antiguos Almacenes de Depósito
San José, Avenida del Puerto 🕒 10.00–18.00

Plaza Carlos III It's no Harrods, but with shops, bars and restaurants
over three levels this is as big and brash as shopping gets in Havana.

ⓐ Avenida Salvador Allende, corner Arbol Seco ⓣ (07) 873 6370
ⓛ 10.00–19.00 Mon–Fri, 09.30–18.30 Sat, 10.00–13.00 Sun

TAKING A BREAK

Café O'Reilly £ ❶ Get a table on one of the balconies and watch the street life while recharging your batteries with a sandwich, steak or chicken kebab. ⓐ O'Reilly no. 203 between Cuba & San Ignacio ⓣ (07) 863 6684 ⓛ 09.00–22.30

Café Santo Domingo £ ❷ The café is on the first floor of the San José bakery, so choose eclairs, *señoritas*, *caracoles* or other sweet delicacies downstairs to accompany a cup of strong

ⓞ *Stop for a breather at one of the cafés in front of the cathedral*

La Bodeguita del Medio is still a popular place

Cuban coffee. There's also a variety of snacks, pizzas and pastas. ⓐ Obispo no. 161 between Mercaderes & San Ignacio ⓣ (07) 860 9326 ⓛ 08.00–00.00

Cafetería Torre La Vega £ ❸ This little restaurant could become your favourite lunchtime hangout if you're on a budget or you just like a quiet midday break. Typical Cuban dishes such as *ropa vieja* (shredded meat, literally 'old clothes') are cheap and reasonable. ⓐ Obrapía no. 114 between Mercaderes & Oficios ⓛ 09.00–21.00

Café El Escorial ££ ❹ If you weren't surrounded by the beautiful colonial mansions of Plaza Vieja, this stylish coffee bar would make you feel as though you were in Paris, London or Vienna. ⓐ Mercaderes no. 317, corner Muralla ⓣ (07) 868 3545 ⓛ 09.00–22.00

Hotel Ambos Mundos ££ ❺ The roof terrace of the Ambos Mundos hotel (Hemingway's first Havana residence) is the ideal place for a break from Havana's busy Old Town and a panoramic view over the city and bay. ⓐ Obispo no. 153 ⓣ (07) 860 9530 ⓛ 09.00–23.00

AFTER DARK

RESTAURANTS & PALADARES
La Bodeguita del Medio ££ ❻ The fact that Ernest Hemingway frequented the Bodeguita makes it one of Havana's top tourist spots – consequently, it's always crowded and slightly overpriced.

The collection of celebrities' photos and signatures, a menu of decent Cuban dishes or just your affection for Hemingway might still justify a call here. ⓐ Empedrado no. 207 between Cuba & San Ignacio ⓣ (07) 867 1374 ⓛ 12.00–00.00

Los Nardos ££ ❼ Habaneros love this traditional Spanish-style eatery, run by a youth association with links to the Asturias region in Spain. Pick *gazpacho Andaluz* (cold tomato and vegetable soup), Spanish tortilla or a generous portion of the main courses. Prepare to queue. ⓐ Paseo de Martí no. 563 between Brasil & Dragones (under the arcades opposite the Capitol) ⓣ (07) 863 2985 ⓛ 12.00–00.00

Paladar Doña Blanquita ££ ❽ This *paladar* has a fantastic location on the Paseo del Martí (El Prado), so try to grab a table on the balcony. ⓐ Paseo de Martí no. 158 between Colón & Refugio ⓣ 867 4958 ⓛ 12.00–00.00

Restaurante La Dominica ££ ❾ A fine Italian restaurant in a pedestrianised area next to the Edificio Santo Domingo, the site of the original university in Havana. A good choice if you need a break from traditional Cuban food. ⓐ Corner O'Reilly no. 108 & Mercaderes ⓣ (07) 860 2918 ⓛ 12.00–00.00

La Taberna de la Muralla ££ ❿ Beer drinkers will be thrilled by this Austrian-Cuban pub on Plaza Vieja, the only place in Havana to serve home brews. The chicken, pork, lobster and fish kebabs, prepared on the outside grill, are particularly popular. ⓐ Corner San Ignacio & Muralla ⓣ (07) 866 4453 ⓛ 12.00–00.00

BARS, CLUBS & LIVE MUSIC

The noisy bars in downtown Calle Obispo attract tourists and *jineteras* (female hustlers) alike. Check out, in particular, **La Dichosa** (ⓐ Corner Obispo & Compostela ⓛ 09.00–12.00), **La Lluvia de Oro** (ⓐ Obispo no. 316 ⓛ 09.00–00.00), **Café París** (ⓐ Corner Obispo & San Ignacio ⓛ 12.00–00.00) and **Bosque Bologna** (ⓐ Obispo no. 460 ⓛ 09.00–00.00).

El Floridita One of the town's landmarks and yes, full of tourists. However, you shouldn't miss sipping a Papa Hemingway in the company of the writer's life-size statue. ⓐ Corner Obispo no. 557 & Monserrate ⓣ (07) 867 1299 ⓦ www.floridita-cuba.com ⓛ 11.30–23.45

Bar Monserrate Good live music in the evening makes this a great place for an aperitif. ⓐ Corner Avenida de Bélgica & Obrapía ⓣ (07) 860 9751 ⓛ 12.00–00.00

Casa de la Música Centro Habana Salsa addicts are in heaven here, undoubtedly the hottest spot when it comes to moving your hips to the rhythms of Cuba's best salsa bands. The cheaper matinée performances are crowded with locals whereas the night performances are more exclusively for tourists. An absolute must! ⓐ Avenida de Italia no. 225 between Concordia & Neptuno ⓣ (07) 862 4165 ⓦ www.egrem.com.cu ⓛ 17.00–21.00, 23.00–03.00 Sun–Fri, 17.00–21.00, 23.00–06.00 Sat. Admission charge

El Louvre The alfresco bar on the ground floor of Hotel Inglaterra is a good starting point for a long Havana night. ⓐ Paseo de Martí no. 416 ⓣ (07) 860 8596 ⓦ www.gran-caribe.com ⓛ 11.00–23.30

Vedado

The literal translation of Vedado is 'forbidden', referring to the fact that in colonial times this used to be a forested area where the felling of trees wasn't allowed. Vedado grew in the late 19th and 20th centuries as a result of wealth generated by the prospering sugar industry, and many splendid mansions were built. Today it is a residential and business district between Central Havana and Playa, which comes alive at night with cabaret shows, nightclubs, Cuba's best jazz club and a top bolero venue. Young Cubans hook up with their friends on the lively Rampa (Calle 23), before diving into one of the live music venues, theatres or cinemas.

This chapter contains three places of interest located south of Vedado but within easy reach: Cementerio de Cristóbal Colon, Plaza de la Revolucion and Teatro Nacional.

SIGHTS & ATTRACTIONS

Cementerio de Cristóbal Colón (Christopher Columbus Cemetery)
With its mausoleums, crypts, chapels, family vaults and religious sculptures, this cemetery can keep you busy for a couple of hours. The list of famous Cubans who found their last home here is endless. Ask at the entrance about guided tours. ❸ Corner Zapata & 12 ❶ (07) 832 1050 ❶ 08.30–16.30. Admission charge

Plaza de la Revolución & Memorial José Martí
Gigantic. What looks at first glance like a product of the Cuban revolution was in fact planned in the 1920s by French landscape

⬤ The towering memorial to José Martí

Straits of Florida

Boca de la
Chorrera

N

............POI
i ....Information
............Police Station
............Airport
............Railway Stn
............Bus Station
............Hospital

PLAZA TEXTO
GARCIA

Estadio
José Martí

CALZADA

AVENIDA DE LOS PRESIDENTES

Teatro
Amadeo
Roldán

Museo de la
Danza

Galería
Habana

LINEA

Galerías
de Paseo

CALZADA

Sala Teatro
Hubert de Blanck

VEDADO

Teatro
Mella

Museo des
Artes Decorat

Gran
Palenque

LINEA

PASEO

LA RAMPA

Chorrera
Castle

CALLE 23

AVENIDA 23 PATA

Cementerio de
Cristóbal
Colón

Río Almendares

Puente 3ra

ALTURAS
DE MIRAMAR

Viazul
Bus Terminal

SAN ANTONIO CHIQUITO

NUEVO VEDADO

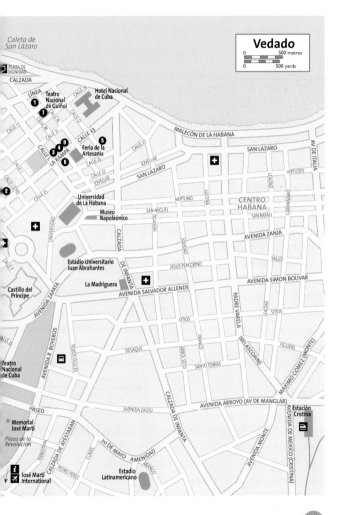

Vedado

0 ———————— 500 metres
0 ———————— 500 yards

Caleta de
San Lázaro

PLAZA DE
DIGNIDAD

CALZADA

LINEA

Teatro
Nacional
de Guiñol

Hotel Nacional
de Cuba

CALLE 39

CALLE I
CALLE H
CALLE M
CALLE 21

CALLE 23

MALECÓN DE LA HABANA

CALLE 27

SAN LAZARO

AV DE ITALIA

Feria de la
Artesanía

LA RAMPA

CALLE G

CALLE D

JOVELLAR

SAN LAZARO

LEALTAD

VIRTUDES

CALLE 25

CALLE 27

JOVELLAR

NEPTUNO

LUCENA

ESCOBAR

CENTRO
HABANA

Universidad
de La Habana

SAN MIGUEL

SAN RAFAEL

CALZADA

HOSPITAL

Museo
Napoleónico

AVENIDA ZANJA

UNIVERSIDAD

DE INFANTA

SOLEDAD

SALUD

Estadio Universitario
Juan Abrahantes

JESUS PEREGRINO

AVENIDA SIMON BOLIVAR

Castillo del
Príncipe

AVENIDA SALVADOR ALLENDE

LEALTAD

SITIOS

La Madriguera

AVENIDA ZAPATA

SITIOS

PADRE VARELA

CALLE 35

FIGURAS

AVENIDA R BOYEROS

POZOS DULCES

DESAGUE

FRANCO

ARBOL SECO

(BELASCOAIN)

MAXIMO GOMEZ (MONTE)

Teatro
Nacional
de Cuba

SANTO TOMAS

CALZADA DE INFANTA

PASEO

AVENIDA ZALDO

AVENIDA ARROYO (AV DE MANGLAR)

Estación
Cristina

AVENIDA DE MEXICO (CRISTINA)

Memorial
José Martí

Plaza de la
Revolución

TERRITORIAL

CALZADA DE AYESTARAN

AVENIDA DE ZANJA

20 DE MAYO

AMENIDAD

AVENIDA MONTE

José Martí
International

PEDRO PEREZ

Estadio
Latinoamericano

ARANGO

EL MALECÓN

The Malecón is Havana's famous 8 km (5 miles) long seaside avenue between Habana Vieja and Chorrera castle at the mouth of the river Almendares. Start at the Castillo de la Punta fort, where you can watch young Cuban daredevils throwing themselves into the sea, and stroll along the avenue taking in the sea views on one side and the fascinating mix of partly collapsing, partly restored houses on the other. Its Habaneros' favourite spot for socialising, so get your people-watching goggles on.

architect Jean Claude Forestier. This is the square where a million people once gathered to listen to Fidel Castro's lengthy discourses. In 1998, Pope John Paul II held a Mass here. The Martí Memorial tower houses a museum dedicated to the national hero. Take the lift up to the top and enjoy the view from one of Havana's highest buildings. ⓐ Plaza de la Revolución ⓣ (07) 859 2347 ⓛ 09.00–16.30 Mon–Sat. Admission charge for museum & tower

Universidad de La Habana (University of Havana)

Originally located in the historic centre, the University of Havana moved to a complex of neoclassical buildings on a hill in Vedado

⬤ *The imposing entrance to the University of Havana*

SÁBADOS DE RUMBA

The acclaimed Conjunto Folklórico Nacional de Cuba performs at 15.00 every other Saturday in the **Gran Palenque** (ⓐ 5 no. 103 between Calzada & 5 ⓣ (07) 830 3060). It's a colourful event, not to be missed by anyone interested in Afro-Cuban music and dance. ⓦ www.folkcuba.cult.cu

---

in 1902. Check out the imposing stairway and the Alma Mater statue of a woman with open arms. ⓐ Corner San Lázaro & L ⓦ www.uh.cu

CULTURE

La Madriguera

A cultural centre, exhibition site, meeting point and venue for Havana's thriving creative scene. The programme here is varied, and includes cutting-edge reggaeton and rap. ⓐ Quinta de los Molinos, corner Calzada de Infanta & Jesús Peregrino ⓣ (07) 879 8175 ⓛ Hours vary depending on event

Museo de Artes Decorativas (Decorative Arts Museum)

Check out how the Cuban bourgeoisie lived before the revolution. Formerly owned by the Counts of Revilla de Camargo, this mansion with its decorated ceilings and walls houses a fascinating exhibition of antique furniture, sculptures and porcelain. ⓐ Corner 17 & E ⓣ (07) 830 9848 ⓛ 10.30–16.30 Tues–Sat ⓦ www.cubarte.cult.cu. Admission charge

Museo de la Danza (Dance Museum)

Located in a beautiful colonial building, this museum is a tribute
to ballet and Cuba's world-famous ballerina Alicia Alonso.
ⓐ Corner Línea & G ⓣ (07) 831 2198 ⓛ 10.00–18.00 Tues–Sun.
Admission charge ⓘ Undergoing renovation at time of writing;
call for updates

Museo Napoleónico (Napoleonic Museum)

Napoleon was in Cuba? No, you didn't miss a historical detail. It's
just that Cuban sugar magnate Julio Lobo was a Napoleon fanatic,
gathering any and every related object that he could get his hands
on and creating the most important collection of Napoleon's
personal belongings in the Americas. There are more than 7,000
items in the collection, all housed in a beautiful Florentine-style
mansion. ⓐ San Miguel 1159 between Masón & Ronda ⓣ (07)
879 1412 ⓛ 09.00–17.30 Tues–Sat, 09.00–13.00 Sun. Admission
charge ⓘ Undergoing renovation; call to check opening hours

Teatro Amadeo Roldán (Amadeo Roldán Theatre)

Destroyed by fire and rebuilt in 1999 as an exact replica of the
neoclassical original, the theatre's two auditoriums are popular
venues for big-name musicians and groups. The National
Symphony Orchestra usually plays on Sundays. ⓐ Corner
Calzada & D ⓣ (07) 832 4835 ⓦ www.cubaescena.cult.cu
ⓛ Box office: 10.30–18.00 Tues–Sun

Teatro Mella (Mella Theatre)

As one of the city's most versatile cultural venues, the Mella
Theatre features dance, music, comedy, and Conjunto Folklórico

Nacional. It also co-hosts the International Ballet Festival (see page 10). ⓐ Línea no. 657 between A & B ① (07) 833 8696, 833 5651 ⓦ www.cubaescena.cult.cu ① Box office: 14.00–18.00 Tues–Sun

Teatro Nacional de Cuba (National Theatre of Cuba)

The Grand Theatre's modern counterpart, this theatre has a busy programme of classical concerts, plays and ballet. If you're suffering from cultural overkill, the Café Cantante Mi Habana (see page 86) below the theatre will bring you back down to earth with hot and spicy salsa. ⓐ Corner Paseo & 39 ① (07) 878 5590 ⓦ www.teatronacional.cult.cu ① 17.00–22.00 Mon–Fri, 16.00–21.00 Sat & Sun

RETAIL THERAPY

Bazar La Habana Sí Get hold of music by Los Van Van or Benny Moré (Cuba's legendary 'Barbarian of Rhythm') at Vedado's best music store. Also sells souvenirs, DVDs and musical instruments. ⓐ Corner L & 23 ① (07) 838 3162 ① 10.00–21.00 Mon–Sat, 10.00–19.00 Sun

Feria de la Artesanía A little street market on Vedado's main Calle 23, specialising in wood, leather and metal craftwork. ⓐ 23 between M & N ① 10.00–18.00 Mon–Sat, 10.00–14.00 Sun

Galerías de Paseo A shopping mall close to Vedado's tourist area and large hotels, where you can get perfume and other luxury goods. ⓐ Corner Paseo & 1 ① (07) 833 9888 ① 09.00–18.00 Mon–Sat, 09.00–13.00 Sun

TAKING A BREAK

Bar La Torre £ ❶ On top of the Focsa building, Vedado's famous restaurant is expensive, so pick the bar instead, order a simple snack and drink and get the same sweeping view over the city for half the price. If you're feeling flush or it's a special occasion, try one of the cocktails. ⓐ Edificio Focsa 33rd floor, 17 no. 55 between M & N ⓣ (07) 838 3088 ⓛ 12.00–23.30

El Cochinito £ ❷ Pork, pork and even more pork is what is served in the Cochinito ('Piggy'). Try the *Bistec Especial Cochinito*, a huge pork chop served with rice, vegetables and salad. ⓐ 23 between H & I ⓣ (07) 832 6256 ⓛ 12.00–22.45 ⓘ Payment in CUP

Coppelia £ ❸ Cubans are crazy for sweets in general and love Coppelia, Havana's close-to-legendary ice-cream parlour, in particular. Prices inside are charged in CUP and there's usually a long queue; to eat your ice cream at the outside tables you have to pay in CUC. ⓐ Corner 23 & L ⓣ (07) 832 6184 ⓛ 10.00–22.00 Tues–Sun

La Rampa Cafetería £ ❹ Located downstairs in the Habana Libre hotel, this is the spot to start and/or end a night out in Vedado. It is open 24 hours and specialises in light meals and fast food – great for a hangover breakfast. ⓐ Corner 23 & L ⓣ (07) 834 6100 ⓛ 24 hrs

Trattoría Maraka's £ ❺ A busy restaurant serving pizzas (some say the best in town), pastas and salads, as well as standard

creole cuisine. It's popular with younger tourists and families.
🅐 Hotel St. John's, O no. 260 between 23 & 25 📞 (07) 833 3740
🕐 10.00–23.00

AFTER DARK

RESTAURANTS & PALADARS

El Mandarín £ ❻ Come here for Cuban-Chinese cuisine at
Cuban peso prices. The two-person *Arroz Frito Especial* is
a protein feast with chicken, pork, ham and large prawns.
🅐 Edificio ICRT, corner 23 & M 📞 (07) 832 0677 🕐 13.00–23.00
Tues–Sun ❶ Payment in CUP

La Casona de 17 ££ ❼ Housed in a beautiful mansion from
the 1920s, the Casona de 17 has creole cuisine, mixed grills and
international dishes on its menu. They claim to serve the best
Arroz con Pollo a la Chorrera (rice with chicken) on the island.
🅐 17 no. 60 between M & N, opposite the Focsa building
📞 (07) 838 3136 🌐 www.palmarescuba.com 🕐 09.00–11.00,
12.00–00.00

Paladar Gringo Viejo ££ ❽ Serves huge plates of excellent Cuban
food with an exquisite touch. *Cordero Estofado*, lamb cooked in
red wine with olives and green peppers, is a popular choice. The
little restaurant is hidden away behind an iron gate. 🅐 21 no. 454
between E & F 📞 (07) 831 1946 🕐 12.00–23.00 Mon–Sat

El Polinesio ££–£££ ❾ The Habana Libre's other (pricier) eating
spot serves night owls hankering after Asian and international

◔ *Lively entertainment at Cabaret Parisien*

food. ⓐ Hotel Habana Libre, corner 23 & L ⓣ (07) 834 6100
ⓛ 12.00–00.00

BARS, CLUBS & LIVE MUSIC

Café Cantante Mi Habana Located downstairs at the National
Theatre (see page 82), this cool dance club has regular live
salsa acts on its programme. The matinée performances
are less touristy. ⓐ Corner Paseo & 39 ⓣ (07) 878 4275
ⓦ www.egrem.com.cu ⓛ 17.00–21.30 Tues–Sun, 23.00–03.00
Thur–Sun. Admission charge

Café Concert Gato Tuerto The bohemian 'One-Eyed Cat' bar,
restaurant and concert venue is Cuba's prime bolero venue

CABARET

If your stay doesn't include a trip to Tropicana (see page 99),
consider one of the (more affordable) shows in Vedado. Good
choices are: **Cabaret Parisien** (ⓐ Hotel Nacional, corner 21
& 0 ⓣ (07) 836 3564 ⓦ www.hotelnacionaldecuba.com
ⓛ 21.00–02.00), **Cabaret Copa Room** (ⓐ Hotel Riviera, corner
Paseo & Malecón ⓣ (07) 836 4051 ⓦ www.gran-caribe.com
ⓛ 21.30–03.30 Thur–Sun), **Cabaret Salón Rojo del Capri**
(ⓐ Corner 21 & N ⓣ (07) 833 3747 ⓦ www.palmarescuba.com
ⓛ 22.00–04.00) and **Cabaret Turquino** (ⓐ Hotel Habana Libre,
corner 23 & L ⓣ (07) 834 6100 ⓦ www.solmeliacuba.com
ⓛ 20.00–03.00 Mon–Sat). All charge an entry fee.

and, although it is a little cramped, it has a decidedly nostalgic atmosphere. The restaurant upstairs is more elegant and offers fixed-price menus. ⓐ O no. 14 between 17 & 19 ⓣ (07) 838 2696 ⓛ Restaurant: 12.00–00.00; bar: 22.00–04.00 Mon–Fri, 20.00–04.00 Sat & Sun. Admission charge for bar

Café Fresa y Chocolate Located at the Cuban Institute of Cinematographic Arts and Industry (ICAIC), this cool terrace bar is the place to spot Cuban actors, filmmakers and other art folks. There are live music gigs and a popular trova night on the last Thursday of the month. Needless to say, it's named after the famous Cuban film *Fresa y Chocolate* (see page 135). ⓐ 23 between 10 & 12 ⓣ (07) 836 2096 ⓛ 12.00–01.00 Tues–Sun. Admission charge

Café TV A popular comedy and cabaret venue with occasional karaoke nights and live concerts. The restaurant serves inexpensive burgers, pastas and salads so you can come here early and not have to budge all evening. ⓐ Corner 17 & N ⓣ (07) 834 4499 ⓛ Restaurant: 12.00–20.30; cabaret: 20.30–03.30. Admission charge for cabaret

Hotel Nacional Don't miss a visit to this historic hotel, scene of heavy fighting in 1933 and subsequently chosen as venue for one of the world's biggest mafia conferences. The Cabaret Parisien (see box opposite) is legendary, but if you're not into dancing ladies the hotel's other restaurants and bars are open to non-guests. A drink in the courtyard bar, overlooking the Malecón

● *The Hotel Nacional offers a range of evening entertainment*

at sunset, is the best choice. ⓐ Corner 21 & O ⓣ (07) 836 3564
ⓦ www.hotelnacionaldecuba.com ⓛ Hours vary but there is
usually something open

Jazz Café Located in a modern shopping mall, the Jazz Café lacks
the smoky-dark-basement ambience one expects from a cool jazz
club. Nevertheless it's one of Havana's top venues for quality
jazz, and serves good cocktails and food. Note that there is a
minimum consumption charge of CUC$10 – otherwise you have
to pay an admission fee. ⓐ Galerías de Paseo, corner Paseo & 1
ⓣ (07) 838 3302 ⓛ 12.00–02.00

Jazz Club La Zorra y el Cuervo Jazz enthusiasts are in for a
feast at Cuba's no. 1 jazz club, located in a cellar that occasionally
gets a bit – well – smoky. The walls are covered in pictures of
jazz legends past and present, from all around the world.
ⓐ 23 between N & O ⓣ (07) 833 2402 ⓛ 22.00–02.00.
Admission charge

Piano Bar Delirio Habanero On the fourth floor of the National
Theatre (see page 82), discover this elegant piano/jazz bar with
an excellent view over Revolution Square. You can order light
meals or just soak up the calm atmosphere. There are often
matinée performances at 15.00, great for a rainy day or a break
from sightseeing. ⓐ Teatro Nacional de Cuba, corner Paseo & 39
ⓣ (07) 878 4275 ⓛ 16.00–20.00 Wed–Sun, 22.00–03.00 Tues–Sun.
Admission charge

Playa & Marianao

Cross the Almendares river to the west and you'll enter the
wealthy area of Miramar, where many embassies, diplomats and
expats have settled. Not surprisingly, *paladares* and upmarket
state-run restaurants have clustered here on the seaside First
Avenue. Miramar is part of the sophisticated district of Playa,
which boasts 12 km (7½ miles) of coastline, decent facilities for
fishing and diving, several high-class hotels, *casas particulares*
in attractive buildings and good restaurants.

South of Playa lies Marianao, which has a reputation for
being a rather tough neighbourhood – however, it has gained
worldwide fame for its splendid 70-year-old cabaret venue
Tropicana and is well worth a visit for this reason alone.

SIGHTS & ATTRACTIONS

Acuario Nacional (National Aquarium)

Children love the dolphin and sea lion shows at this fun aquarium,
which displays a variety of fish and sea life. Plans are in the
pipeline to create an educational marine park and centre for
marine biodiversity. ❸ Corner Avenida 3 & 62 ❶ (07) 202 5872
ⓦ www.acuarionacional.cu ❶ 10.00–18.00 Tues–Sun.
Admission charge

Club Habana

Dive into a distinguished country club with a private beach,
swimming pool, sports and recreation centre, sauna, gym and
shops. In pre-revolutionary times, this was the grand Biltmore

Yacht & Country Club. Day passes are available for non-members.
ⓐ Avenida 5 between 188 & 192 ❶ (07) 204 5700 ⓦ www.cpalco.com.
Admission charge

◆ *Spectacular acrobatics at the National Aquarium*

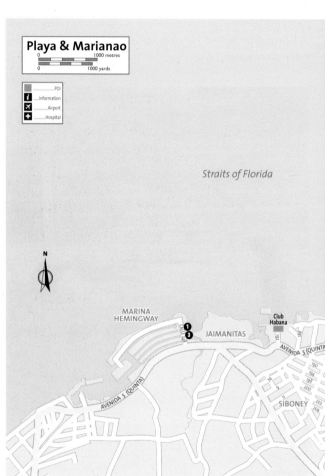

Playa & Marianao

| 0 | | 1000 metres |
| 0 | | 1000 yards |

- POI
- *i* Information
- ✈ Airport
- ✚ Hospital

Straits of Florida

N

MARINA HEMINGWAY

❶❸

JAIMANITAS

Club Habana

AVENIDA 5 (QUINTA)

AVENIDA 5 (QUINTA)

SIBONEY

MIRAMAR

Teatro
Karl Marx

Chorrera
Castle

Playita de la
Calle 16

Pabellón para la
Maqueta de la
Capital

LA SIERRA

Casa de la
Música

Acuario
Nacional

Galería
Comercial
Comodoro

Fundación Antonio
Jiménez de la
Naturaleza y el Hombre

Iglesia
Jesús de
Miramar

ALMENDARES

Salón Rosado
Benny Moré

PLAYA

La Isla del
Coco

BUENAVISTA

Tropicana

MARIANAO

CUBANACÁN

VERSALLES

LOS
ANGELES

LA CORONELA

José Martí
International

AUTOPISTA DEL ESTE

Marina Hemingway

Want to catch a big fish? Charter a fishing boat at the Marina Hemingway, Cuba's main nautical centre at the western end of Playa. There's also a diving centre for scuba and snorkelling, along with elegant restaurants, bars and a beach. Havana's *jeunesse dorée* ('golden youth', or rather rich kids) like to hang out here.

Pabellón para la Maqueta de la Capital (Scale Model of the Capital Pavillon)

A 22 m by 10 m (72 ft by 33 ft) scale model of Havana, which illustrates how the city has developed over the centuries. It is one of the world's largest scale models of a city and well worth

HAVANA'S FIFTH AVENUE

Quinta Avenida, just like its namesake in New York, is Havana's most upmarket street. The main artery in Playa, it is not a shopping destination, but a wide, tree-fringed avenue with splendid mansions lining both sides, many occupied by foreign embassies, businesses and local authorities. If you have got used to Habana Vieja and Centro Habana's narrow, crowded streets, here you will see the city from quite a different angle. On Quinta you'll pass Cuba's biggest church, the Iglesia Jesús de Miramar – only the dome of the Capitol is bigger – as well as the truly monumental Russian embassy. The avenue heads west towards Marina Hemingway, a great place to stop for lunch.

⬤ *Paradise is a Miramar beach*

a visit. ⓐ 28 no. 113 between Avenidas 1 & 3 ⓣ (07) 202 7303
🕐 09.30–17.00 Mon–Sat. Admission charge

Playita de la Calle 16

The rather rocky 'Little Beach of Street 16' in Miramar is popular
among young Cubans who want a quick swim after work without
having to drive too far. Don't expect sophisticated beach facilities,
but there's a kiosk selling you ice-cold beers and other refreshments.
ⓐ Corner Avenida 1 & 12, 14 & 16

CULTURE

Fundación Antonio Nuñez Jiménez de la Naturaleza y el Hombre (Antonio Nuñez Jiménez Foundation for Nature & Humanity)

A fascinating collection of items amassed by Cuban scientist

Antonio Nuñez Jimenez during a trip from the source to the mouth of the Amazon. ⓐ Avenida 5B no. 6611 between 66 & 70 ⓦ www.fanj.org ⓛ 09.00–16.00 Mon–Fri. Admission charge

RETAIL THERAPY

La Casa del Habano A branch of the famous House of the Cigar which has a dedicated tobacco-tasting room. ⓐ Corner Avenida 5 & 16 ⓣ (07) 204 7973 ⓦ www.lacasadelhabano.cu ⓛ 11.00–23.00

Egrem Tiendas de Música State-run recording company Egrem sells its Cuban CDs, instruments and accessories at various stores in Playa. Tienda Casa de la Música Miramar: ⓐ Corner Avenida 35 & 20 ⓣ (07) 204 1980 ⓛ 09.00–21.00; Tienda de 18: ⓐ 18 between Avenidas 1 & 3 ⓣ (07) 204 1978 ⓛ 09.00–17.00 Mon–Sat; Tienda de Quinta y 88: ⓐ Avenida 5 between 86 &88 ⓣ (07) 204 8759 ⓛ 10.00–17.00 Mon–Fri

Galería Comercial Comodoro One of Havana's biggest and most upmarket malls, with shops such as Mango, Adidas, Converse, Benetton and Clarks. ⓐ Avenida 3 between 80 & 84 ⓣ (07) 204 6177 ⓛ 09.00–19.00 Mon–Fri, 09.00–14.00 Sun

TAKING A BREAK

Pain de París £ ❶ As the name suggests there is some French know-how involved at this bakery. Pop in for a croissant and coffee while soaking up Marina Hemingway's holiday atmosphere.

ⓐ Marina Hemingway, corner Avenida 5 & 248 ⓣ (07) 204 7628
ext 737 ⓛ 08.00–21.00

El Palenque £ ❷ Even posh Playa has its cheap eateries, and the
Palenque is one of them. Under open-air thatched huts you can
tuck into pizzas, pastas, grills, *pollo frito con congrís* (fried chicken
with rice and beans) and *langosta* (lobster). ⓐ Corner 17 & 190
ⓣ (07) 271 8167 ⓛ 11.30–22.00

Pizza Nova £ ❸ Using only natural ingredients for their pizzas
and pastas, this Italian restaurant claims to be one of the best
in town. ⓐ Marina Hemingway, corner Avenida 5 & 248
ⓣ (07) 204 6969 ⓛ 12.00–00.00

AFTER DARK

RESTAURANTS & PALADARES
El Aljibe ££ ❹ Try the excellent creole house speciality *pollo Aljibe*
– roast chicken served with fried plantains and yuca (cassava)
with *mojo*, a delicious sauce of bitter orange and garlic. It has
been on the menu for years and you can eat as much as you like.
ⓐ Corner Avenida 7 & 26 ⓣ (07) 204 1583 ⓛ 12.00–00.00

Don Cangrejo ££ ❺ *Cangrejo* (crab) is the speciality here, but
you can enjoy other seafood dishes along with a glass of wine
and a magnificent view over the Straits of Florida. If you need to
cool down, jump into the swimming pool (best done before rather
than after dinner). ⓐ Avenida 1 between 16 & 18 ⓣ (07) 204 3839

🕐 Restaurant: 12.00–00.00; pool: 10.00–18.00; live music: 22.00–03.00 Fri & Sat

Dos Gardenias ££ ❻ A fun complex with Italian, Chinese and Cuban restaurants to choose from. If you're feeling frisky, head to the Salón Bolero after dinner. ⓐ Corner Avenida 7 & 26 ☎ (07) 204 9517 🕐 Restaurants: 12.00–00.00; Salón Bolero: 22.30–01.30 Sun–Thur, 22.30–03.00 Fri & Sat

Paladar Mi Jardín ££ ❼ Up for something hot and spicy? 'My Garden' offers genuine Mexican food cooked by a Mexican chef. Try *pollo mole poblano* (chicken with chocolate sauce) or feast on quesadillas, enchiladas and the obligatory tacos. ⓐ 66 no. 517 between Avenida 5B & 7 ☎ (07) 203 4627 🕐 12.00–00.00

Paladar Los Cactus de 33 £££ ❽ Your wallet will be a lot lighter after dining at this exclusive Miramar paladar, but your stomach will be pleasantly full of Cuban cuisine at its best and you'll be happy with the professional, efficient service. ⓐ Avenida 33 no. 3405 between 34 & 36 ☎ (07) 203 5139 🕐 12.00–00.00

Paladar La Fontana £££ ❾ The Fontana aroused international interest with good reviews in prestigious magazines. Start off at the Yerbabuena tapas bar, then move to the restaurant for fish and meat grills, chargrilled octopus with pesto, homemade sausages and tamales. ⓐ Corner Avenida 3 & 46 ☎ (07) 202 8337 🌐 www.lafontanahavana.com 🕐 12.00–00.00

TROPICANA

Get a glimpse of Cuba's *Diosas de Carne* ('Flesh Goddesses', as the showgirls are known) at the legendary Tropicana in Marianao. Open since 1939, it was run by Cuba's 1940s and 50s mafia as a casino and cabaret welcoming showbiz celebs such as Nat King Cole and Carmen Miranda. Known as the 'Paradise under the Stars', the show hasn't lost any of its glamour today. Come early for a drink in the 1950s-style cocktail bar Café Rodney or a meal in Restaurante Los Jardines, housed in the former casino. ⓐ 72 between 41 & 45 ⓘ (07) 267 1717 ⓦ www.cabaret-tropicana.com ⓛ Cabaret: 20.30–01.00; restaurant: 19.00–23.00; bar: 12.00–00.00. Admission charge for show

🔺 *The legendary Tropicana*

BARS, CLUBS & LIVE MUSIC

Casa de la Música Miramar Located in a former freemason mansion, this is the laid-back twin sister of the 'House of Music' in Central Havana. Los Van Van, Adalberto Alvarez y su Son and all the other big names of Cuban music perform regularly here. ⓐ Corner Avenida 35 & 20 ⓣ (07) 204 0447 ⓦ http://promociones.egrem.co.cu ⓛ 17.00–21.00, 23.00–04.00

El Diablo Tun Tun Above Casa de la Música Miramar is another venue hosting regular live music acts. ⓐ Corner Avenida 35 & 20 ⓣ (07) 204 0447 ⓛ 17.00–21.00, 23.00–06.00 ⓦ http://promociones.egrem.co.cu

Sala Atril In the Karl Marx theatre, the 150-capacity Sala Atril club conveniently combines a restaurant and cocktail bar with an intimate live music venue. ⓐ Teatro Karl Marx, corner Avenidas 1 & 10 ⓦ www.cpalco.com ⓣ (07) 206 7596 ⓛ Opening hours depending on event type

Salón Rosado Benny Moré (Tropical) The Salón, known locally as La Tropical, is a fantastic open-air venue: when Cuba's best salsa and son groups start playing the dance floor trembles with young Cubans shaking their booty. Come for the Sunday matinée if you want to dance with locals rather than tourists – a genuine Cuban experience. ⓐ Corner Avenida 41 & 46 ⓣ (07) 206 4799 ⓛ 21.00–01.00 Fri, 21.00–02.00 Sat, 15.00–21.00 Sun (matinée). Admission charge

---

ⓞ *Lush foliage and bulbous hills in the Viñales Valley*

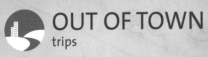

OUT OF TOWN
trips

Towards Playas del Este

By the time you've walked your feet off in Habana Vieja and danced the night away in salsa and jazz clubs, you'll be covered in blisters and ready for another holiday. So now it's time to relax and head east to the sandy, palm-lined beaches and crystalline waters of the Playas del Este. Spend at least an afternoon here, but preferably a couple of days – there are some good *casas particulares* in Guanabo.

The Playas del Este are crammed full with locals in July and August, and fairly touristy between December and March, but you

can come here at any time. In summer in Guanabo, you'll find yourself in an almost totally Cuban environment, whereas parts of Santa María del Mar have a higher percentage of foreign tourists. Facilities at the beaches are fairly underdeveloped, but that gives them all their charm and authenticity. Rest assured that a cold beer, a mojito or a daiquiri are always in sight and a decent number of good restaurants and snack bars will keep you from starving.

The various beaches are all connected, so if you're feeling energetic you can take a long walk or early morning run along the seaside from El Mégano to Guanabo beach.

The expansive white sandy beach of Santa María del Mar

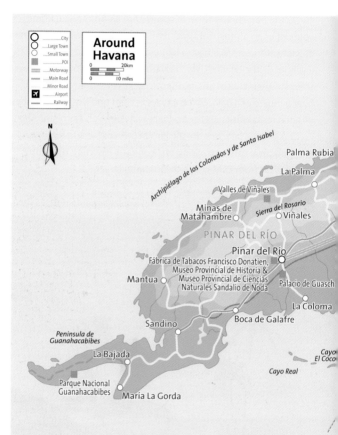

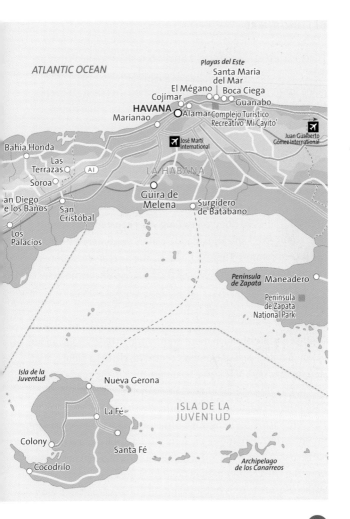

GETTING THERE

There is currently no efficient public transport to the Playas del Este, except for one Víazul bus (see page 50) per day; however, plans are in the pipeline to make this more frequent so check Ⓦ www.viazul.cu for updates. If you don't have a hire car, you will probably have to take a taxi.

SIGHTS & ATTRACTIONS

Boca Ciega
A small, palm-fringed beach west of Guanabo. There are no tourist facilities so bring everything you need with you. Views over palms, sand and aquamarine waters do compensate for the lack of comfort. There is, however, the nice, air-conditioned Restaurante El Cubano (see page 110) just across the meadow behind the beach.

Cojímar
Cojímar is still not much more than a little fishing village about 10 km (6 miles) east of Havana's centre. Its claim to fame is that Hemingway kept his fishing boat here back in the 1940s and 50s (see page 108). Cojímar immortalised their beloved 'Papa', as Cubans affectionately call the author, with a gilded bust; you'll also come across Hemingway's (supposedly) favourite restaurant, La Terraza de Cojímar (see page 110). If you stroll around the harbour you'll spot the Torreón de Cojímar, a Spanish fort dating from the 17th century. In 1994 Cojímar gained fame once again, as the site where tens of thousands of Cubans, frustrated with

⬥ *Nice spot of beach life at Guanabo*

THE OLD MAN AND THE SEA
Cojímar is yet another of Havana's Hemingway-once-hung-out-here spots. In those days it was just a little fishing village where the writer and passionate fisherman kept his boat, *El Pilar*. The village was also home to Gregorio Fuentes, Hemingway's friend and captain of *El Pilar*. It was Fuentes who supposedly inspired the writer for his book *The Old Man and the Sea*. Although Fuentes lived in Cojímar until he died at the age of 104 in 2002, it is said that he never read the famous book.

the terrible economic situation of the Special Period, boarded anything floating to cross the Straits of Florida in the hope of a better life in the US.

Guanabo
Guanabo, at the eastern end of the beaches, used to be a little fishing village but is now developing an infrastructure of restaurants, bars, nightclubs and shops. The beach itself is popular with locals in summer, although two big tumbledown buildings right on the central beach leave no doubt that Guanabo's tourism potential still has a long way to go. There are various small hotels of varying quality, but your best bet if you want to make the most of the beaches is to seek out one of the nice *casas particulares* in the village. At any rate you should definitely have a meal at Paladar El Piccolo (see page 111), one of the best Italian restaurants in and around Havana.

El Mégano

A kilometre-long beach crowded with locals in summer, with a café-restaurant, sun loungers and parasols for rent and water sports facilities in season.

Santa María del Mar

Santa María del Mar is the longest and the most beautiful of the beaches in this area, with the highest concentration of hotels and tourist facilities. Parallel to the coastline runs the Avenida de las Terrazas, with a good choice of restaurants, snack bars and mini supermarkets. Santa María beach is lively and busy with both tourists and locals, and there's always live music or something going on at the beach bars. The **Complejo Turístico Recreativo 'Mi Cayito'** (ⓐ Avenida de las Terrazas, Itabo ① (07) 797 1339 ① 10.00–18.00) has a restaurant and some pedal boats in which you can paddle around the small lagoon.

RETAIL THERAPY

Come to the Playas del Este to sunbathe, not shop. Apart from a few mini-supermarkets, the biggest shopping metropolis in the area is the small and fairly unexciting **Galería Comercial Guanabo** (ⓐ Corner Avenida 5 between 466 & 468, Guanabo ① (07) 796 3811 ① 09.00–19.00).

TAKING A BREAK

Cafeteria Vía Blanca £ The Vía Blanca offers typical Cuban dishes including chicken, pork, beef and a variety of seafood such as

lobster, shrimps and fish.  Hotel Via Blanca, Avenida 5 between 486 & 488, Guanabo ● (07) 796 3183 ● 24 hrs

Restaurante Mi Cayito £ A lovely outdoor restaurant on a little island in Laguna Itabo, specialising in seafood and creole cuisine. Try the *arroz con mariscos* (rice with seafood, similar to Spanish paella) or *zarzuela*, a local dish prepared with fish, lobster and shrimps. ● Laguna Itabo, Avenida de Las Terrazas, Santa María del Mar ● (07) 797 1339 ● 10.00–18.00

La Terraza de Cojímar ££ If you decided to pay tribute to Hemingway and make a stop in Cojímar this is the obligatory place to have lunch. 'La Terraza' was allegedly the writer's favourite tavern and it still serves some good seafood dishes such as fish soup and paella. If you're feeling brave, try the daiquiri Hemingway. ● Corner Real no. 161 & Candelaria, Cojímar ● (07) 766 5151 ● Restaurant: 12.00–23.00; bar: 10.30–23.00

AFTER DARK

RESTAURANTS & PALADARES
Restaurante El Cubano £ Cool down from the beach in the nice air-conditioned ambience of this restaurant and enjoy creole cuisine such as *ropa vieja* (shredded meat). The restaurant operates a 24-hour outdoor snack bar. ● Avenida 5 between 454 & 458, Boca Ciega ● (07) 796 4061 ● Restaurant: 11.00–23.00; snack bar: 24 hrs

Restaurante Mi Casita de Coral £ Withdraw from the beach to this little restaurant for good value seafood as well as Cuban and international dishes. ⓐ Corner Avenida las Banderas & Avenida de las Terrazas, Santa Maria del Mar ⓣ (07) 797 1602 ⓛ 10.00–22.00

Paladar Maeda ££ It's worth the uphill climb to get to this excellent *paladar*, which serves generous plates of Cuban and international food. If the mosquitoes behave themselves, you can also dine alfresco. ⓐ Quebec no. 115 between 476 & 478, Bello Monte, Guanabo ⓣ (07) 796 2615 ⓛ 18.00–23.00

Paladar El Piccolo ££ Locals come all the way from the city centre to this Italian-influenced *paladar* to enjoy pizzas baked in a wood stove and authentic *al dente* pasta. Book in advance. ⓐ Avenida 5 between 502 & 504, Guanabo ⓣ (07) 796 4300 ⓛ 12.00–00.00

BARS, CLUBS & LIVE MUSIC

Cabaret Guanimar An unpretentious, open-air music venue with occasional live acts by small or up-and-coming groups. Check the programme for show times. ⓐ Avenida 5 between 466 & 468, Guanabo ⓣ (07) 796 2947 ⓛ 21.00–03.00 Wed–Sun. Admission charge

Guanabo Club You have spent your day on a most marvellous beach, so don't be too picky when night falls – Guanabo nights aren't Vedado nights! However, this is a decent spot for one last drink before hitting the sack. ⓐ 466 between 13 & 15, Guanabo ⓣ (07) 796 2884 ⓛ 22.00–03.00. Admission charge

Relax on the sandy beach or enjoy poolside activities at Hotel Atlántico

ACCOMMODATION

Aparthotel Las Terrazas £ Apartments with one, two or three rooms, equipped with refrigerators, air conditioning and satellite TV. Breakfast is included and it is only a stone's throw away from the Santa María del Mar beach. Within the complex are restaurants, bars, a swimming pool and a little shop. ⓐ Avenida de las Terrazas between 10 & Rotonda, Santa María del Mar ⓣ (07) 797 1344 ⓦ www.islazul.cu

Hotel Atlántico ££ An all-inclusive hotel right next to the beach, with a swimming pool, tennis courts, gym, restaurants and a disco. You can hire kayaks and catamarans during the day and take part in Latin American dance classes at night. There's a free shuttle service to the city centre three times a day. ⓐ Avenida de las Terrazas, Santa María del Mar ⓣ (07) 797 1085 ⓦ www.hotelesc.com

Tropicoco ££ This reasonably priced, all-inclusive hotel offers a twice-daily shuttle service to the city centre, a swimming pool and regular live entertainment in the evenings. ⓐ Corner Avenida Sur & Avenida de las Terrazas, Santa María del Mar ⓣ (07) 797 1371 ⓦ www.hotelesc.com

Villa Los Pinos ££ An attractive complex of houses with two, three or four rooms and a kitchen. Most have their own swimming pool. ⓐ Avenida de las Terrazas, Santa María del Mar ⓣ (07) 797 1361 ⓦ www.hotelesc.com

Towards Valle de Viñales

Pinar del Río, the country's tobacco-growing province southwest of Havana, is easily accessible as a day trip or overnight stay. It is known as the 'Garden of Cuba' for a reason, luring lovers of nature and outdoor activities with its waterfalls and natural swimming pools, its myriad bird species (including the *tocororo*, Cuba's national bird) and its opportunities to get into the great outdoors. You can visit abandoned coffee plantations, browse one of the world's biggest orchidariums, enjoy the offerings of

● *The spectacular landscape of the Valle de Viñales in Pinar del Rio province*

Las Terrazas, Cuba's first eco-resort, or discover the unique Viñales Valley on the back of a horse.

GETTING THERE

Víazul (see page 50) operates one bus service per day to Viñales, stopping at Pinar del Río on the way. The total journey takes three and a quarter hours and doesn't give you the freedom to do much sightseeing. If you only have a day to spare, it's best to book a bus tour through one of the travel agencies in Havana (see page 134).

SIGHTS & ATTRACTIONS

Pinar del Río

The provincial capital is not a must-do stop on your trip through Pinar del Río, but it does contain the interesting **Fábrica de Tabacos Francisco Donatien** (ⓐ Maceo 157 🕐 09.00–16.00 Mon–Fri, 09.00–12.00 Sat & Sun), a tobacco factory and the city's prime tourist attraction. There are also a couple of small museums (see page 120).

San Diego de los Baños

Well known for its natural mineral springs, this little town 130 km (81 miles) southwest of Havana is a pleasant place to stop on your journey. The old spa resort **Balneario San Diego** (🕐 (048) 778 338) has been undergoing extensive renovation work; if you are into mud baths and massages, call them to check whether it has re-opened.

POLO MONTAÑEZ

The eco-community of Las Terrazas (see page 118) produced its own celebrity in the form of the late singer and songwriter Polo Montañez. With just two CDs under his belt, his hit song *Un Montón de Estrellas* ('Loads of Stars') catapulted the so-called *guajiro natural* (natural countryman) to fame. He died tragically in a car accident at the age of only 47. **La Casa de Polo** (🕐 09.00–17.00), a small museum dedicated to the singer, is a major attraction in Las Terrazas.

◯ *Pinar del Rio cathedral*

A few kilometres west of San Diego is the fairly run-down Parque La Güira, and just north of this is the Cueva de los Portales. Che Guevara chose this cave as headquarters of the Western Army during the Cuban Missile Crisis, and a small museum now contains some of his belongings. Opening hours of the museum are highly variable, so stop at the small campsite about a kilometre away from the cave to check.

Soroa

The natural paradise of Soroa is just a few kilometres southwest of Las Terrazas (see below) and also part of the Sierra del Rosario. There are various hiking trails and opportunities for bird-watching, but the area's main attraction is a botanical garden with a magnificent **Orchidarium** (🕒 08.30–17.00) containing more than 700 types of orchid. The Salto de Soroa waterfall plunges more than 20 m (66 ft) into the Manantiales river.

Las Terrazas

Around 50 km (31 miles) from Havana on the way to Pinar del Río is the eco-tourism resort of Las Terrazas. The area, covered by coffee plantations of French-Haitian immigrants in the 19th century, was run to ruin by short-sighted agricultural techniques in the early 20th century. In an effort to improve this situation, terraces (*terrazas*) were built and the area reforested. Las Terrazas was founded as a model settlement and the area around it was declared Cuba's first UNESCO-sanctioned biosphere reserve, the Sierra del Rosario.

You can explore Las Terrazas by foot, bicycle, on the back of a horse, and even 'by air' – i.e. a canopy zip-slide. There are trekking and biking tours of various levels of difficulty (ask at the information centre in Rancho Curujey, see page 122), and a host of rich flora and fauna to discover. Those who prefer a morning coffee to an energetic hike can visit the historic ruins of French coffee plantations at **Cafetal Buenavista** (🕒 11.30–15.00), which houses a small museum and a restaurant.

Whether you choose to tour or trek, afterwards you can relax with a swim in the San Juan River or one of the lakes, recharge your batteries at one of the complex's eateries (see page 122) and then visit the community's art studios. ⓐ Autopista Habana–Pinar del Río km 51, Candelaria ⓣ (048) 578 555 ⓦ www.lasterrazas.cu

🔺 *Eco-settlement Las Terrazas*

Valle de Viñales (Viñales Valley)

Viñales Valley, a UNESCO World Heritage site since 1999, is one of Cuba's most beautiful landscapes. Its unique geology is formed by mogotes, limestone hillocks covered with vegetation which arise abruptly from the flat, fertile, green land. The same agricultural techniques are used to cultivate tobacco here as they were centuries ago.

If you book an excursion in Havana you will be taken to the excellent vantage point at Horizontes Los Jazmines hotel (see page 124) for a photo session. If you travel here independently, you could spend a night at a *casa particular* in the picturesque Viñales village and then explore the valley by foot, horseback or by taking one of the tours offered by local agencies in the village.

Typical side-trips in the valley include the **Cueva del Indio** (Indian's Cave ● 09.00–17.00), a cave system more than 1.5 km (1 mile) long, and the Mural de la Prehistoria, a fairly unimpressive mural painted onto a rock.

CULTURE

Museo Provincial de Ciencias Naturales Sandalio de Noda (Sandalio de Noda Natural Science Museum)

The Palacio de Guasch, Pinar del Río's fanciest building, now houses a natural science museum with samples of Cuba's endemic flora and fauna and interesting insect and butterfly collections. The dinosaur skeletons are its main attraction.
ⓐ Martí no. 202 between Comandante Pinares & Hermanos Saíz, Pinar del Río ● (048) 753 087. Admission charge ● Undergoing renovation at time of writing; call for updates and opening times

Museo Provincial de Historia (Provincial History Museum)
This museum depicts the history of the Pinar del Río province
and exhibits, among other things, archeological finds dating
back to Indian settlements in pre-Columbian times. There are
also some personal items relating to Enrique Jorrín, the genius
behind the cha-cha-cha. ⓐ Martí no. 58 between Isabel Rubio y
Colón, Pinar del Río ⓣ (048) 724 272 ⓛ 08.30–18.30 Tues–Sat,
09.00–13.00 Sun. Admission charge

RETAIL THERAPY

Bazar el Cusco Exhibition space of the local artists' community,
where you can view and buy some of their works. ⓐ Las Terrazas
ⓛ 10.00–18.00

Casa del Habano A branch of the nationwide cigar shop with all
the famous brands, plus a pleasant smokers' lounge and a little
café. ⓐ Antonio Maceo no. 157 between Plaza de la Independencia
& Rafael Morales, Pinar del Río ⓣ (048) 778 122 ⓛ 09.00–17.00
Mon–Fri, 09.00–12.00 Sat

La Casa del Ron At the 'House of Rum' you can buy a whole variety
of Cuban rums as well as souvenirs such as t-shirts. ⓐ Antonio
Maceo no. 151 between Galiano & Antonio Taraza, Pinar del Río
ⓣ (048) 778 002 ⓛ 09.00–17.00 Mon–Fri, 09.00–12.00 Sat

El Ilang Take some of Las Terrazas' scent with you. Flowers, roots
and leaves are processed to make natural fragrances at this little
shop. ⓐ Las Terrazas ⓛ 10.00–18.00

TAKING A BREAK

La Fonda de Mercedes £ Owner Mercedes serves up typical local dishes on the terrace next to her house, which has a marvellous view over Las Terrazas. @ Las Terrazas ● 09.00–21.00

Rancho Curujey £ Enjoy lunch in the relaxing ambience of this bar-restaurant on the banks of the El Palmar lake. The Rancho serves typical creole dishes and also has a useful information centre where tours can be booked. @ Las Terrazas ● (048) 578 700 ● 09.00–21.00

Ranchón Soroa £ Located at the Horizontes Villa Soroa hotel, this restaurant is open to anyone looking for a quick bite to eat. @ Carretera de Soroa km 8, Candelaria ● (048) 523 534 ● 10.00–22.00

AFTER DARK

As well as the options below, a good choice for dinner is Las Terrazas' eco-hotel Moka (see page 124).

Restaurante Vera ££ At this restaurant, located at the Horizontes Los Jazmines hotel, you can order dishes à la carte or take your pick from a buffet. @ Carretera de Viñales km 25 ● (048) 796 205 ● www.cubanacan.cu

El Romero ££ At this upscale eco-restaurant in Las Terrazas everything is made from fresh organic ingredients. Great choice for vegetarians. @ Las Terrazas ● 09.00–22.00

La Terraza **££** The terrace of Hotel Ermita is one of the best places to eat in the Viñales region. Not only do you have marvellous views over the valley, but the food, *comida criolla*, is delicious.
ⓐ Carretera La Ermita km 1.5, Viñales ❶ (048) 796 071
ⓦ www.cubanacan.cu ⓛ 07.15–10.00, 12.00–14.30, 19.00–22.00

ACCOMMODATION

Horizontes Villa Soroa **£** Charming little two-room bungalows. Facilities include two restaurants, five bars and a swimming pool. ⓐ Carretera de Soroa km 8, Candelaria ❶ (048) 523 534
ⓦ www.hotelescubanacan.com

◔ *Relax at the sweet Horizontes Villa Soroa*

Hotel Mirador £ If you'd like to enjoy the warm thermal waters of the San Diego Spa (see page 116) for more than a day, get a room at this nearby hotel. You should check that the spa is definitely open for visitors before making a booking.
ⓐ 23 & Final, San Diego de los Baños ⓣ (048) 778 338

Horizontes Los Jazmines ££ From the hotel's belvedere you can gaze over the whole valley. The misty early morning view is particularly beautiful. There is a good restaurant, Restaurante Vera (see page 123), on site. ⓐ Carretera de Viñales km 25
ⓣ (048) 796 205 ⓦ www.hotelescubanacan.com

Hotel Moka ££ An eco-hotel in the midst of Las Terrazas' forested hills, and the perfect starting point for nature-based activities. Facilities include a swimming pool, tennis court, restaurant and tour booking desk. ⓐ Las Terrazas ⓣ (048) 578 600
ⓦ www.lasterrazas.cu

plaza
Joaquín de Agüero ↑

plaza de la
Solidaridad ↑

parque
José Martí  ↑

plaza
← **San Juan de Dios**

plazuela del
← **Puente**

parque
← **Ignacio Agramonte**

PRACTICAL
information

Directory

GETTING THERE

By air

There are frequent flights to Havana's José Martí International Airport (see page 46) from European cities including London, Paris, Madrid and Amsterdam. Due to the US embargo there are currently no commercial flights from the US to Cuba, so the best option is to come via Mexico or Canada (see see pages 127–8 for travel restrictions on US citizens). Note that on leaving Cuba you will be required to pay an Airport Departure Tax of CUC$25 (in cash). Cuba's national airline Cubana de Aviación offers direct flights to the UK and other destinations. Airlines to check are:

Air Europa Ⓦ www.aireuropa.com
Air France Ⓦ www.airfrance.com
Cubana de Aviación Ⓦ www.cubana.cu
Iberia Ⓦ www.iberia.com
KLM Ⓦ www.klm.com
Virgin Atlantic Ⓦ www.virgin-atlantic.com

Many people are aware that air travel emits CO_2, which contributes to climate change. You may be interested in the possibility of lessening the environmental impact of your flight through **Climate Care** (Ⓦ www.climatecare.org), which offsets your CO_2 by funding environmental projects around the world.

By road

Havana is connected to other major Cuban cities by a long-distance bus service operated by Víazul (see page 50). Hiring a car (see page 54) is the most convenient way of getting around the island. Fearful drivers should beware, however, that road maintenance leaves a lot to be desired, signage is generally insufficient, and lighting at night virtually nonexistent. Driving is on the right and speed limits are 50 km/h (31 mph) in the city, 90 km/h (55 mph) on ordinary roads (*carreteras*) and 100 km/h (62 mph) on motorways (*autopistas*).

ENTRY FORMALITIES

All tourists visiting Cuba must have a passport valid for at least six months after the trip and a visa known as a *Tarjeta de Turista* (Tourist Card). These are sold by airlines and travel agencies and are valid for 30 days (with one month's extension possible within Cuba), except for Canadian citizens whose cards are valid for 90 days. Due to the current embargo, the majority of US tourists

🔺 *All nationalities are welcomed at José Martí International Airport*

are officially not allowed to travel to Cuba unless they have a licence obtained in advance from US authorities. If they do (through a third country such as Canada or Mexico) they could face severe consequences once back in the US. There are no restrictions on them from the Cuban authorities. Cuban-Americans with close family in Cuba can now travel back and forth between the two countries as often as they like.

Tourists can bring in most objects needed for personal use, including photo and video cameras, portable musical equipment, radios, TVs, laptop computers and DVD players. It is, however, strictly forbidden to bring along any form of satellite communication, including GPS systems and satellite phones. Plants and animal and vegetable products (including fresh fruit) are not allowed to be brought into the country. The usual duty-free allowances regarding alcohol and tobacco are in place.

On departure, if you are taking more than 50 cigars out of the country you must have the receipt(s) proving that you purchased them in a state-run shop. To take valuable artworks home with you, you usually need a special export stamp (ask for this when purchasing at art shops and stalls). The amount of cash you can legally take out of the country is limited to CUP100 and CUC$200.

For more customs information and up-to-date notices and limits, see ⓦ www.aduana.co.cu.

MONEY

Cuba has two currencies. Cuban Pesos (CUP), also called *moneda nacional* (national currency) are used by locals to buy basic goods. Cuban Convertible Pesos (CUC) are used for luxury goods and for payment in tourist establishments, including hotels, tourist

🔺 *Cuba has two currencies*

restaurants, most shops and taxis. Both currencies are broken down into 100 centavos. CUC$1 is roughly equivalent to US$1 while CUP$1 is worth less than 4 US cents.

The easiest way to get hold of either currency is to change money at banks and in *cadecas* (exchange offices). Bring along euros, pounds sterling, Swiss francs or Canadian dollars. US dollars are subject to a penalty fee. You can also withdraw CUC from ATMs, which are fairly plentiful in Havana. However, they are not always reliable and they are much harder to find in rural areas. If leaving the city make sure you have a supply of cash on you. Note also that withdrawing cash using a credit or debit card incurs a 12.5 per cent charge. Credit cards are not widely accepted except in upper-end establishments, where MasterCard, Visa and Diners Club cards can be used if they are not issued in the US. No US credit cards are currently accepted in Cuba.

HEALTH, SAFETY & CRIME

Havana is a safe city for foreign visitors and Cuba is generally a safe country. Take the normal precautions, such as watching your personal belongings in crowded areas or on the beach. Police patrols are frequent in tourist areas.

Hygiene is good in most restaurants so eating fruit and vegetables shouldn't cause any problems. You should drink bottled rather than tap water and avoid ice in lower-quality establishments. It helps to have a small supply of your usual stomach settler medicine with you, just in case.

All visitors must have proof of comprehensive travel and/or medical insurance from an official Cuba-accredited company before arrival, or will be forced to purchase it at the airport. Be wary of visiting ordinary hospitals, which suffer from a lack of funding. On the other hand, Havana has some first-class medical institutions (it is a destination for health tourism) which can be contacted in case of emergency or for a consultation. See page 136 or ask at your hotel for recommendations. There are a few international pharmacies in town (including at the Hotel Habana Libre, see page 36), but you are best advised to carry a first aid kit and your usual painkillers and other medicines in your luggage.

OPENING HOURS

Shops are generally open 09.00–17.00 Monday to Saturday and 09.00–14.00 on Sundays. Office hours are weekdays from 08.30 or 09.00–17.00 or 17.30, usually with a lunch break and a tendency to knock off early. Banks close earlier, at around 15.00. Museums are usually open 10.00–18.00, with some closing on Mondays. Restaurants open from 12.00–00.00 with slight variations.

TOILETS

The availability of (well equipped) toilets is a problem in Havana. There are no public toilets except in museums, restaurants and bars. There is usually an attendant who will give you a few sheets of toilet paper in return for a coin (around 20 CUC centavos is sufficient). Soap, running water, baby-changing facilities and wheelchair-accessible toilets are all luxuries that are generally unavailable.

CHILDREN

Havana's vibrant lifestyle, friendly locals and warm weather make it a good place to bring children. Apart from building sandcastles and playing in the sea, there are many activities that will keep them (and you) amused. If you're lucky you'll bump into the Zanqueros de Habana Vieja, a group of street artists in fancy dress and on stilts, who perform around the Plaza de Armas. The puppet theatre at **Teatro Nacional de Guiñol** (ⓐ Edificio Focsa, M between 17 & 19, Vedado ⓣ (07) 832 6262) is superb for children of all ages.

Small children will have fun playing in the **Parque La Maestranza** (ⓐ Peña Pobre between Tacón & Carlos Manuel de

Céspedes ⏰ 09.00–17.00. Admission charge), while older children can appreciate the small **Aquarium** (ⓐ Brasil No. 9 between Mercaderes & Oficios ⏰ 09.00–17.00 Tues-Sun. Admission charge) just around the corner from Plaza Vieja.

The National Aquarium (see page 90) with its dolphin shows is always an attraction – and if you're already out there in Miramar you might as well visit **La Isla del Coco** (ⓐ Avenida 5 & 112, Playa ☎ (07) 208 3003 ⏰ 14.00–18.00 Fri, 10.00–20.00 Sat & Sun, Sept–June; 10.00–20.00 Wed–Sun, Jul & Aug. Admission charge) the biggest amusement park in Havana.

COMMUNICATIONS
Internet
Internet cafés aren't prolific in Havana, but bigger hotels have internet access in their lobbies and some also offer Wi-Fi. The most central public internet café is Cibercafe Capitolio, inside the Capitol (see page 60). Cuba's national phone company ETECSA operates two 'Telepunto' call centres with internet access. One is in Habana Vieja (ⓐ Habana No. 406 between Obispo & Obraría) and one is in Centro Habana (ⓐ Corner Aguila No. 565 & Dragones). Both are open 08.30–19.30 daily. Just don't expect a high-speed connection.

Phone
At ETECSA's Telepunto subsidiaries (see above) you can make national and international phone calls as well as send and receive faxes, print, scan and photocopy. They also sell phone cards for use in public ETECSA phone boxes. You can buy cards in either CUP or CUC, but remember that only cards paid for in

TELEPHONING HAVANA

To call Cuba from abroad, dial your country's international calling code (00 from the UK, 011 from the US) followed by 53 for Cuba, then 7 for Havana, then the seven-digit local number.

TELEPHONING ABROAD

To make an international call from Cuba dial 119, followed by the relevant county code, the area code (usually dropping the first zero if there is one) and the local number you require. Country codes include: Australia 61; New Zealand 64; Republic of Ireland 353; South Africa 27; UK 44; US 1.

CUC can be used to phone abroad. Using a mobile phone in Cuba is prohibitively expensive.

Post

Stamps can be bought in post offices (*Oficinas de Correos*), hotel receptions and some shops that sell postcards. Be prepared for it to take several weeks for your letters and cards to arrive.
Oficina de Correos La Habana Vieja ⓐ Oficios No. 102, at entrance to Plaza de San Francisco de Asís 🕐 08.00–18.00 Mon–Sat

ELECTRICITY

The Cuban electricity system operates with 110/120 volts, 60 hertz and uses flat two-pin plugs. Luxury hotels might have outlets with 220 volts – ask at reception. UK and European appliances will require a plug adaptor, which you can usually buy at your departure airport.

TRAVELLERS WITH DISABILITIES

Cuba's infrastructure is not great for wheelchair users and travellers with other severe disabilities, since many older buildings have steps, awkward corners and no lifts, ramps or accessible toilets. However, upper-range hotels and the more modern or newly-restored buildings should be more accessible. It may be a good idea to book through a tour company (see below), making sure that your exact needs are understood. If travelling independently, take a reliable companion with you and don't be afraid to ask locals for help if needed. The main organisation for people with disabilities in Cuba is **Asociación Cubana de Limitados Físico-Motores** (@ 6 No. 106 between Avenidas 1 & 3, Playa ((07) 202 5070 www.aclifim.sld.cu).

TOURIST INFORMATION

Cuba's official tourist information service is **Infotur** (@ Obispo No. 524 between Bernaza & Villegas, Habana Vieja ((07) 866 3333 www.infotur.cu 08.30–17.30). There are branches at the airport, Miramar and Guanabo. Almost all big hotels in Havana have a desk for one of the main travel agencies where both guests and non-guests can book various city tours and excursions. Some reliable agencies are:

Cubanacán @ 17A No. 71 between 174 & 190, Playa ((07) 208 9920 www.cubanacanviajes.cu

Cubatur @ Corner 23 & L, Vedado ((07) 833 3142 www.cubatur.cu

Havanatur 🄰 Complejo Hotelero Neptuno-Tritón, Corner 3 & 74, Miramar ☎ (07) 201 9800 🄦 www.havanatur.cu
San Cristóbal 🄰 Oficios No. 110 between Lamparilla & Amargura, Habana Vieja ☎ (07) 861 9171

Useful websites

Popular unofficial websites about life in Cuba and Havana include 🄦 www.cubaabsolutely.com, 🄦 www.cubalinda.com and 🄦 www.thehmagazine.com. For listings of cultural events and live music, check 🄦 www.cubarte-english.cult.cu or the Spanish-only 🄦 http://promociones.egrem.co.cu.

BACKGROUND READING & FILMS

Buena Vista Social Club, a film by Wim Wenders. A beautiful, moving documentary about the musical encounter of US guitar player Ry Cooder with Cuban legends Compay Segundo, Ruben González, Ibrahim Ferrer and Omara Portuondo.
Dirty Havana Trilogy by Pedro Juan Gutiérrez. One of the most interesting examples of recent Cuban literature, this novel takes you into a world of alcohol, drugs and sex in today's Havana.
Fresa y Chocolate (Strawberry and Chocolate), a film by Tomás Gutiérrez Alea. A humorous, Oscar-nominated film depicting the friendship of two men.
The Old Man and the Sea by Ernest Hemingway. Essential reading by Cuba's most famous resident author.
Our Man in Havana by Graham Greene. The satirical espionage tale is set in the time of Batista's regime.
Suite Habana, a film by Fernando Pérez. A silent documentary film showing the double life of many Cubans.

Emergencies

The following are emergency numbers:

Ambulance ☎ 838 1185 or 838 2185

Fire ☎ 105

Police ☎ 106

Asistur (@ Paseo de Martí no. 208 between Trocadero & Colón (Habana Vieja) ☎ (07) 866 4499 ⓦ www.asistur.cu ⏰ 24 hrs) is an agency which assists foreigners in emergencies including medical assistance and evacuation, lost luggage and documents or legal assistance.

MEDICAL SERVICES

You are obliged to take out (and have proof of) comprehensive health cover from an officially approved insurance company before arriving. If you fall ill while in Cuba, you should visit an international private hospital or clinic.

Clínica Central Cira García (@ 20 No. 4101, corner Avenida 41, Playa ☎ (07) 204 2811 ⓦ www.cirag.cu) is an international clinic offering 24-hour emergency treatment as well as general consultations and an international pharmacy. You can also turn to the **Hospital Nacional Hermanos Ameijeiras** (@ San Lázaro No. 701, off Malecón, Centro Habana ☎ (07) 876 1000).

POLICE

There is a strong police presence in Havana. Police wear a distinctive dark blue uniform and cap. In the case of theft, contact the police to file a report (*hacer una denuncia*) and obtain a police statement (*declaración*) for your insurance.

EMERGENCY PHRASES

Help!	**Fire!**	**Stop!**
¡Ayuda!	¡Incendio!	¡Pare!
¡Ayoodah!	*¡Eensendyoh!*	*¡Pareh!*

Call an ambulance/a doctor/the police/the fire service!
¡Llame a una ambulancia/a un médico/a la policía/
a los bomberos!
¡Yameh ah oona amboolancya/ah oon medeekoh/
ah la policya/ah los bomberos!

Policía Nacional Revolucionaria (PNR) 🇦 Picota between Paula
& San Isidro, Habana Vieja ☎ (07) 861 9110 🕐 24 hrs

EMBASSIES & CONSULATES
The Republic of Ireland and New Zealand have no representation
in Cuba – the nearest embassies are in Mexico. Australian citizens
in difficulty should contact the Canadian embassy.
Canada 🇦 Corner 30 No. 518 & Avenida 7, Playa ☎ (07) 204 2516
🌐 www.canadainternational.gc.ca/cuba
South Africa 🇦 Corner Avenida 5 No. 4201 & 42 ☎ (07) 204 9671
🌐 www.dfa.gov.za
UK 🇦 34 No. 702 between Avenida 7 & 17, Playa ☎ (07) 214 2200
🌐 http://ukincuba.fco.gov.uk
US Interests Section 🇦 Calzada between L & M, Vedado
☎ (07) 833 3551 🌐 http://havana.usint.gov

ABOUT THE AUTHOR

An avid traveller, writer and researcher, Nina Stampfl was born in Austria and worked variously for publishing companies, international organisations and government ministries before moving to Mexico City in 2006. Her lifelong passion for Latin America was confirmed when she married her Cuban husband in 2005. Although still based in Mexico, she travels regularly to Havana, where she loves to seek out the hottest new places to hear Cuban music and dance salsa.

Editorial/project management: Lisa Plumridge
Copy editor: Monica Guy
Layout/DTP: Alison Rayner

The publishers would like to thank the following individuals and
organisations for supplying their copyright photographs for this book:
bernavazqueze, page 95; BigStock.com (Roxana Gonzalez, pages 102–3;
Chris Howey, page 75; Mike Lee, pages 19 & 62; Aleksandr Palmero,
page 47; Alexander Yakovlev, page 55; Dušan Zidar, page 29); Bit Boy,
page 43; Chris Brown, page 40; Wagner T Cassimiro "Aranha", pages 25,
70 & 78–9; Nick Castle, page 53; Fidel Castro/Fotolia.com, page 91;
James Emery, page 119; Roxana Gonzalez/Fotolia.com, page 9; David
Grant, pages 34–5; Tony Hisgett, pages 16, 45 & 57; Hoteles C, page 112;
R W Jamieson, page 21; Christopher Lancaster, page 99; Laura, page 123;

Send your thoughts to
books@thomascook.com

- **Found a great bar, club, shop or must-see sight that we don't feature?**
- **Like to tip us off about any information that needs a little updating?**
- **Want to tell us what you love about this handy little guidebook and more importantly how we can make it even handier?**

Then here's your chance to tell all! Send us ideas, discoveries and
recommendations today and then look out for your valuable input
in the next edition of this title.

Email the above address (stating the title) or write to:
pocket guides Series Editor, Thomas Cook Publishing, PO Box 227,
Coningsby Road, Peterborough PE3 8SB, UK.

WHAT'S IN YOUR GUIDEBOOK?

Independent authors Impartial up-to-date information from our travel experts who meticulously source local knowledge.

Experience Thomas Cook's 165 years in the travel industry and guidebook publishing enriches every word with expertise you can trust.

Travel know-how Thomas Cook has thousands of staff working around the globe, all living and breathing travel.

Editors Travel-publishing professionals, pulling everything together to craft a perfect blend of words, pictures, maps and design.

You, the traveller We deliver a practical, no-nonsense approach to information, geared to how you really use it.

Marco, pages 107 & 117; neiljs, page 64 & 69; Nikki Price, pages 125 & 129; Mark Rowland, pages 33 & 88; Rodrigo Sala, page 101; Matthias Schack, pages 114–15; Brian Snelson, pages 13 & 85; sputnik, page 127; SXC.hu (Jordi Calvís Burgués, page 5; franksag, pages 7 & 67; Francisco Jurado, pages 38–9; Crystal Woroniuk, page 60).

Useful phrases

English	Spanish	Approx pronunciation
BASICS		
Yes	Sí	*Sí*
No	No	*Noh*
Please	Por favor	*Por fabor*
Thank you	Gracias	*Gratheeas*
Hello	Hola	*Ola*
Goodbye	Adiós	*Adeeos*
Excuse me	Disculpe	*Deeskoolpeh*
Sorry	Perdón	*Pairdohn*
That's okay	De acuerdo	*Dey acwerdo*
I don't speak Spanish	No hablo español	*Noh ahblo espanyol*
Do you speak English?	¿Habla usted inglés?	*¿Ahbla oosteth eengless?*
Good morning	Buenos días	*Bwenos dee-ahs*
Good afternoon	Buenas tardes	*Bwenas tarrdess*
Good evening	Buenas noches	*Bwenas notchess*
Goodnight	Buenas noches	*Bwenas notchess*
My name is ...	Me llamo ...	*Meh lliamo ...*
NUMBERS		
One	Uno	*Oono*
Two	Dos	*Dos*
Three	Tres	*Tres*
Four	Cuatro	*Cwatro*
Five	Cinco	*Thinco*
Six	Seis	*Seys*
Seven	Siete	*Seeyetey*
Eight	Ocho	*Ocho*
Nine	Nueve	*Nwebey*
Ten	Diez	*Deeyeth*
Twenty	Veinte	*Beintey*
Fifty	Cincuenta	*Thincwenta*
One hundred	Cien	*Thien*
SIGNS & NOTICES		
Airport	Aeropuerto	*Aehropwerto*
Rail station	Estación de trenes	*Estatheeon de trenes*
Platform	Vía	*Veea*
Smoking/ Non-smoking	Fumadores/ No fumadores	*Foomadoores/ No foomadoores*
Toilets	Servicios	*Serbeetheeos*
Ladies/Gentlemen	Señoras/Caballeros	*Senyoras/Kaballieros*
Bus	Guagua	*Gwa-gwa*